COMMUNICATING:
A Pastor's Job

Volume 1: Basics

Robert D. Kendall
MDiv. PhD.

BOBALU Publications
St.Cloud, Minnesota

Communicating: A Pastor's Job
Volume 1: Basics

Copyright © 1995 by Robert D. Kendall

Printed in the United States of America

Published by BOBALU Publications
2578 14 1/2 Avenue SE St. Cloud, MN 56304

ISBN 0-9647504-0-6

First Edition

Cover Design: Nancy Jean Schram
Printing: Sentinel Printing, St. Cloud, MN

Table of Contents

A Special Acknowledgement

It is impossible to acknowledge everyone who has contributed indirectly to this book. Though I must take final responsibility for its content and for the perspective behind it, I also recognize that what is written here is the product of relationships that span more than half a century. Without these other people and all they have given me of themselves, whatever I say here would only be "groundless book-learning" based on someone else's theories.

Most of all, I want to acknowledge the part LuBell, my loving wife and best friend for more than forty years, has played in my struggle to understand human communication. She has demonstrated the virtue of patience far and beyond whatever was said and/or implied in our marriage vows. She listened to thirteen years of Saturday night run-throughs of my sermons. She worked while I went to school, and still had time to be a "sounding board" for my ideas and papers. She's always been there when I needed a "shoulder to cry on," and she's allowed me the privilege of being her shoulder when she's needed one. She's listened to my excitement, excuses, and frustrations over the past eight years of developing and writing this book. And now we're working out together this thing called "retirement" which sometimes casts a whole new light on communication.

I should also acknowledge the important part my children, all mature adults now, have had in my understanding of human communication. Each of the four has contributed significantly to who I am and what I know about human behavior. They, too, have exhibited great patience as their father struggled to find out who he was and where he was going. Keith, Dean, and John also have found themselves in the teaching profession and deeply involved in their respective churches, and KarenLu successful in the business field where communication skills are more than a luxury. As I wrote this book, experiences with each of them kept flashing through my mind, some illustrations probably long forgotten except by Dad. I hope it won't cause any sibling tension to express a special appreciation to John, who is acting as my editor for this book, and who continues to exhibit extreme patience as he tries to teach me the capabilities of this continually-changing instrument called the computer.

Others I might acknowledge, colleagues in the ministry and in academia, parishoners and students, my seminary and graduate school professors, my parents, daughters-in-law, grandchildren—all greatly appreciated and who deserve to be acknowledged as having considerable influence on my life and understanding of human communication—will have nice things said about them in whatever future works I complete.

Preface

Many times during my thirteen years in the pastorate I wished for some kind of quick-reference manual to which I might refer for just the right word or phrase to help me through a tight spot with someone, or to help me cope with a tension-wrought relationship. If there only existed on my bookshelves, or better yet in my suitcoat pocket or in the lining of my robe, a body of indexed communication strategies guaranteed to work wonders as I interacted with the people of my parish, I could be a more effective (and happier!) pastor.

On my bookshelves were numerous volumes on preaching, written by homileticians, and many helpful books on counseling, written by psychologists. Though many of these works were of great value, and I frequently referred to them, and though I might have wished preaching and counseling were the only responsibilities I had, in reality these two functions did not consume the majority of my time.

How *did* I spend the largest segment of time in those sixty to ninety hour weeks as a pastor? What did I do for hours on end while I waited to fulfill my "weightier" responsibilities as a pastor? I related to people. I interacted with them. (Except when I could legitimately "bury" myself in my study with my blessed books!) Most of this was done on a less-than-formal basis, although there were all those interminable committee meetings, too.

I longed for that magic book of pithy sayings which would enliven conversations, move along committee meetings that dragged, smooth ruffled feathers, challenge the overly comfortable, comfort (without sounding trite) those who hurt, or even to inspire the person who had lost hope. Why didn't someone write a book that would do all these things?

Now I realize such a book would be impossible to write, and this is not an attempt to do so. Rather, it is an attempt to connect what I've learned in over twenty years of teaching speech communication in college to what I wish I had known during those first thirteen years as a pastor in a local church.

In this two volume work, I will be taking an interpersonal communication approach to each of the subjects and situations I attempt to cover. At the beginning of each chapter I will identify a verse and/or passage from Scripture (from the New Revised Standard Version) that illustrates some aspect of the subject, as an example of that communication interaction. Throughout, I will include models, diagrams, pictures, and graphics gleaned from the most applicable communication research available, sprinkling the text with illustrations and examples from common parish situations. Since I consider this somewhat of a "fieldtext," I have purposely included numerous lists for quick reference and skill-building, and I apologize to any reader who may find such listing intrusive, distracting or offensive.

Volume One (Chapters One through Nine) covers the "Basics" of communication. These chapters are preceded by a "Pre-Minichapter," an attempt to ground the work and the reader in the most essential component of ministry: commitment. Chapter One lays the foundation for understanding the following chapters, as it provides definitions and the underlying communication theory for this approach to the work of a pastor. Chapters Two and Three look at self-concept and the process of perception as the bases for all human communication. Chapters Four and Five cover the use of language and nonverbal behavior as the vehicles of communication. Chapters Six through Nine discuss selected skills for more effectively using those vehicles of communication: listening, self-disclosure, handling defensiveness, and conflict management.

Volume Two (Chapters Ten through Fifteen) will discuss "Situations" in which communication occurs, plus taking a look at the subject of "ethics." Chapters Ten through Thirteen delve into the problems and possibilities of generalized communication situations: informal conversations, interpersonal relationships, working in small groups, and public speaking. Briefly discussed in Chapter Fourteen will be four specific interpersonal situations which demand special communication skills: power situations, communicating within the organization, male/female communication, and family relationships. Chapter Fifteen will overview the subject of ethics in communication as an aid in better understanding both the pastor's and the layperson's behavior and responsibility. A caution should be inserted at this point. Even though a reader, because of a particular communication crisis, might be most interested in one of the subjects discussed in Volume Two and tempted to read it first, I suggest that not be done. Volume Two is being written with the assumption that Volume One has been read first, because what is said there not only describes my approach to communication, it also explains many references I make in Volume Two. Not that it would be impossible to gain anything from reading Volume Two by itself, only that reading Volume One first would make more sense out of Volume Two.

As mentioned above, these volumes are not meant to be classroom textbooks (although they could be used as such, particularly in connection with the seminary field-work requirement), but rather "fieldtexts" for men and women already in the pastorate and for those who someday hope to be. They may well be helpful, also, to lay ministers and to others involved in the many aspects of pastoral work, from church staff members to volunteer committees. Although a number of skills are discussed, these two small volumes are not meant to be primarily for skill development, a goal that can only be met satisfactorily through human interaction and practice in a classroom or workshop environment. Rather, these books have been written as a guide for readers to better understand what occurs when human beings attempt to communicate. Hopefully, *from this understanding* will come *a more effective use* of those communication skills we already possess, and, coupled with a few new skills suggested here, each reader will enjoy a more fulfilling and successful ministry.

Pre-Minichapter
First Things First

"As he walked by the Sea of Galilee, he saw two brothers, Simon, who is called Peter, and Andrew his brother, casting a net into the sea—for they were fishermen. And he said to them, 'Follow me, and I will make you fish for people.' Immediately they left their nets and followed him."

Matthew 4:18-20 NRSV

"As Jesus was walking along, he saw a man called Matthew sitting at the tax booth; and he said to him, 'Follow me.' And he got up and followed him."

Matthew 9:09 NRSV

"Then he said to them all, 'If any want to become my followers, let them deny themselves and take up their cross daily and follow me.'"

Luke 9:23 NRSV

"The next day Jesus decided to go to Galilee. He found Philip and said to him, 'Follow me.'" John 1:43 NRSV
"Whoever serves me must follow me, and where I am, there will my servant be also."

John 12:26a NRSV

The reason I've called this a "pre-minichapter" is because of an assumption I'm making which undergirds every chapter that follows. Simply stated: A complete understanding of the communication process will only be a cerebral activity, and all the communication skills in the world will sound hollow, forced, or artificial, and consequently ineffectual, if they do not flow from a pastor's personal commitment to the Faith. If the pastor has not answered the call to "Follow me," as Jesus so frequently states in our Scriptures, then everything that is printed in this book, even though studiously read and conscientiously practiced, will sooner or later be perceived by others as only so much "sound and fury, signifying nothing."

Every theological argument, however well reasoned and presented; every emotional appeal, however strongly made; every psychological insight, however personally helpful, will eventually lose its communicative power if the pastor is ever perceived as "inauthentic;" that is, if the source of the argument or appeal or insight is viewed as shallow and rootless and not personally committed to the point being made—in our case, to the Deity whom we worship.

In the past few years we have been made painfully aware of media-preachers who communicate with their television audiences using very persuasive techniques. Many of us have wished that our preaching would be so captivating. Their success has been temporarily phenomenal; but the emphasis, I believe, should be on the "temporarily" rather than on the "phenomenal" part of their success. With all of their understanding of how to "turn on" an audience in modern-day America, with all the skillfully applied techniques they use in communicating with these audiences, they have largely "fallen from grace." Why? It seems to me that their audiences began to question the preacher's own commitment to the Message being advocated. There was something that was "just not right" with them. Many of these former listeners and followers seemed to know instinctively that having a knowledge of human behavior and being able to apply the techniques of psychological manipulation are not sufficient for the pastor's job of communicating the Gospel. There must be a foundation of personal commitment.

Of course, there is one glaring exception to the above negative perception of many media-preachers. That exception is Billy Graham. Although he did not begin as primarily a media-preacher, but rather as a "stadium-evangelist," I include him in this category because over the years he used the media so effectively as a vehicle for his preaching. Few people have ever questionned his commitment to the Faith. And his communication skill is superb. He knows how to relate to an audience, and he does it effectively.

As a young man in high school wondering what I was going to do with my life, I had the privilege of knowing a wonderful, nearing-retirement, Welch pastor by the name of Tom Williams. As I recall, Rev. Williams was somewhat short on pulpit-communication skills, and his small-group skills may have been a bit wanting, too; but there was absolutely no doubt in my mind, and in the minds of most of his parishioners, that he was committed to the Faith. He exuded a sense of commitment that I wanted to emulate. He didn't *talk* about it so much as he "*walked*" it! Highlighting the influence of Tom Williams on my life is meant in no way to disparage the importance of communication skills in the pastor's work. I do not believe that "all you need is commitment" in order to be an effective pastor. To be sure, Tom would have been a much more effective pastor had he further developed his communication skills. What I do mean to say is that merely understanding the process and developing the skills are not sufficient for the work of a pastor. Commitment to the Faith must come first. It is basic. It is the foundation on which the pastor builds her/his communication skill. It is true that commitment can carry a pastor a long way in the vocation, but without a developed skill in communicating, the vocational goal of exciting others about the Gospel will be greatly limited.

Therefore, as William Bradford wrote in 1647 when describing the daily adventuring of the Pilgrims at Plymouth, "So they committed themselves to the will of God and resolved to proceed," I proceed in writing this "field-text" on communication, recognizing for myself and reminding my readers that commitment precedes the work. "Communicating—A Pastor's Job" requires great skill in daily relationships, skill that can be developed and polished by building an understanding of the process and by continuously practicing more effective communication behavior; however, it must first be rooted and grounded in the pastor's authentic personal commitment. Without this commitment, even the best of skills will eventually evolve into but a toolchest of manipulative techniques.

A Thought Worth Considering:

"Communication is supposed to be the antidote against our solitude. Never before have people had so many ways of communication and education, ways of reaching out to another, and never before have people been so separated. True communication must be embodied—it is an act of incarnation. It must be shared—it is an act of communion. To cut oneself off from others is to disconnect oneself from dialogue with God, with life itself."

—The Rev. John Chryssavgis
Russian Orthodox Church in Australia

Chapter One
Understanding the Process

"'Come, let us build ourselves a city, and a tower with its top in the heavens, and let us make a name for ourselves, lest we be scattered abroad upon the face of the whole earth.' And the Lord came down to see the city and the tower, which the sons of men had built. And the Lord said, 'Behold, they are one people, and they have all one language; and this is only the beginning of what they will do; and nothing that they propose to do will now be impossible for them. Come, let us go down, and there confuse their language, that they may not understand one another's speech.' . . . Therefore its name was called Babel, because there the Lord confused the language of all the earth."

Genesis 11:4-7,9 NRSV

Whether or not this passage is true in fact, it *is* true that we as humans experience the confusion of language, not only the difficulty to communicate between languages, but also within the same language. "I don't understand you! . . . We don't talk the same language! . . . You're not hearing what I'm saying! . . . We're not communicating!"

Most of us, when we attempt to communicate with someone, expect to be understood. We automatically assume that the image or meaning we have in our head is the same as the one in our listener. When I told the Pastor/Parish interviewing committee, before assuming one pastorate, that I came out of the "liberal" tradition, one member heard the "came out" as having left the liberal tradition, whereas two other members understood "liberal" as socially permissive and couldn't understand why I objected at a later date to their use of the church as nothing but a community social club in which the constraints of the denomination did not apply. I expected them to understand what *I* meant by the term "liberal tradition:" applying the teachings of Jesus to the community and world in which we lived by whatever means we could within the democratic tradition. Then, when they did not live up to my expectation to understand me, nor I to understand them, we were all frustrated and felt somewhat betrayed by the other. Of course, compounding the problem, when we each did not clarify what we meant, but rather assumed by the smiles of acknowledgment that we not only understood but also agreed, we set the stage for a drama of disappointment during the months ahead.

George Shapiro, professor of speech communication at the University of Minnesota, developed four generalizations on communication (as recorded in this author's class notes with a variation subsequently printed in <u>Interpersonal Communication in the Modern Organization</u> by Bormann, Howell, Nichols, and Shapiro), the fourth of which is "The normal result of the communication process is at least partial misunderstanding." This observation of his, based on years of observation and supported by volumes of research from numerous and varied disciplines, contrasts sharply with our natural inclinations and frequent behavior. Whereas we assume the other person will naturally understand what we are saying, Shapiro suggests that the *normal* result of the communication process is not understanding, but at least partial *mis*understanding!

When I was very young, even as early as grade school, I was very "cause-oriented," reacting strongly to any situation in which I perceived there to be an injustice. And I was one who couldn't keep my mouth shut about it! My parents had ingrained in me the attitude that justice frequently needs an advocate and champion. I believe they did a magnificent job in raising their children; however, they did make some mistakes, as many of us do with our children. I remember well one of these mistakes. One day when I returned home from school, I remember it as being in junior high, I was particularly frustrated because some of my classmates either couldn't or wouldn't see my point of view on some social issue having to do with equality and justice. When I complained to my mother, whom I remember as always being willing to listen to my concerns, about their lack of understanding, she gave me a very common bit of

3

advice that over the years has caused me innumerable hours of anxiety and grief: "Bob, if you would only think before you speak, and find exactly the right words to express your feelings, everyone would understand you." So I studied the dictionary for hours on end to improve my vocabulary and to find those "right words." I bit my tongue in silence until those "right words" came to mind. When I did everything just right, so I thought, the results were frequently the same: I was still misunderstood. Why?! Either I must be a poor communicator, or the other person is to blame for being unwilling to work at understanding my words. I never thought to blame the process for being the problem! It wasn't until graduate school at age 37 that I learned the *process* was faulty, that it wasn't necessarily my own ineptness or the other person's recalcitrance that kept us from understanding each other.

Over the years since graduate school that truth has increasingly influenced my behavior. "The normal result of the communicating process is at least partial *mis*understanding." When I participate in any communicating relationship I need to remember that no matter how clearly I express myself, the other person will normally and naturally *mis*understand, and I will need to seek actively my listener's feedback and to check frequently as to what s/he is hearing me say—all in order to reduce the expected misunderstanding which will occur.

Contrast this approach with being in a conversation and expecting the other person naturally to understand. In the latter case I will not work as diligently at communicating my message since understanding of it is expected. When something does go wrong, I will probably blame the other person for putting roadblocks onto the normally uncongested highways of our relationship. Since *I* am sincere and dedicated to the process of conveying my message, and since *I* know what I mean, it really isn't *my* fault if we don't understand each other; so it must be *you*. How simple! How problematical! The act of communicating, a gift from God to bridge the gap between human beings, being used to divide and to isolate! All because we expect the wrong thing! It is the *process*, for whatever reason, that is flawed. The writer of the Genesis account had his perception of why these communication breakdowns occur. We may either accept that story as fact or hold to some other view; the reality is that communication problems *do* occur, and that it is a normal result of the process. Our acceptance of that reality will determine to a large extent the amount of energy we exert in a communication interaction and the amount of frustration we experience from that conversational relationship.

Since we've looked at Shapiro's final generalization on the communication process, I think it would be wise to consider the other three at this point, too. His first generalization is actually his definition of communication at the interpersonal level: "Anytime anyone says or does something, and what s/he says or does or fails to do or say has an effect on interpersonal relationships or the accomplishment of a task, or s/he wants it to have an effect, then the communicating process is occurring." As one of my students once said in class after hearing this definition, " You cannot *not* communicate!"—unsuspectingly repeating an oft-quoted statement. Some of what Shapiro is saying here is that communication is not time-restrictive; it happens all the time and any place. He includes both verbal and nonverbal communication in his definition. Silence or the absence of an utterance can have an effect on someone, and that effect is part of the process of communicating. Even when the other person does not hear, but I want him to do so, *I* am in the process of communicating; in other words, communication does not need to be "complete," that is, "received." Of course, when it is not received, or not received accurately (as I meant it), it is most certainly *ineffective* communication! However, the *process* is still occurring.

"We just don't communicate anymore!" is a statement heard frequently in marriage and family counseling. If Shapiro is correct, and I believe he is, that statement is inaccurate. The family members *are* communicating; however, messages are being garbled, blocked, or misinterpreted. What the persons are saying or not saying to each other is certainly having an effect on their interpersonal relationships; therefore, the communicating process is occurring. When this is understood, the starting place in counseling shifts from laying blame on each other to trying to figure out what is actually being said. After the "real" message is identified, the family members can then be guided through the steps of healing. Until such a time, everyone involved is mired in the deep morass of confusion. (Of course, the attempt to confuse is sometimes used as a defense mechanism or a power play, something we will discuss in a later chapter; however, even here it is true that nothing can be accomplished until the family sorts out what is actually being communicated between them, and stops concluding that they "just aren't communicating.")

The second generalization Shapiro makes is: "Whenever someone deliberately communicates, certain predictions are being made (this is a predictive process)." The reader will note the insertion of the word "deliberately." We all know that inadvertant communication takes place, particularly in the realm of the nonverbal. We may be always communicating, but we are not always *deliberately* communicating. At the conclusion of worship services, in many traditions, the pastor greets members of the congregation, positioning himself/herself where the congregants have convenient access. Occasionally a parishioner will "pass by on the other side," avoiding personal contact with the minister. This is a situation in which deliberate communication is occurring, and certain predictions are being made. The "avoider" may be predicting that the minister will not notice, or not care, or is too busy to talk, or will understand there's a reason which has nothing to do with their relationship (maybe the oven roast needs immediate attention!). The prediction may or may not be accurate; however, it is being made. If the minister is concerned about that particular behavior, and interprets it as some kind of indicator on their relationship (particularly a negative one), s/he might be wise to "check it out." A phone call or a house call might be in order during the upcoming week.

In an administrative board meeting the treasurer suggests that the church delay payment of the pastor's monthly paycheck for a few days so the heating bill can be paid on time. Behind such a suggestion (a deliberate statement) is a prediction. It might be a challenge to the board to organize its priorities; it might be an indicator of ill-feeling and a way to verbalize it with impunity; it might be a plea to the pastor to make such an offer; it could be any one of a host of reasons. Whatever it is, a prediction is being made as to what the response will be, a prediction that may or may not come true.

If it does, the predictor will take a predetermined line of action; if it does not, the predictor will need to adjust to the response, and alter the line of action. In either case, a prediction has been made.

A few years ago while stopped at a traffic-light, I noticed a bumper sticker on the car just in front of me. It read "If you love Jesus, honk!" So I honked. The driver in that vehicle turned around with an angry scowl and "gave me the finger." I had predicted a different response; I was wrong.

When my wife and I would prepare the evening meal after a long day at school, I would sometimes come up behind her, put my arms around her waist and give her an affectionate squeeze. I was predicting she would snuggle back into my arms and respond affectionately, as she did most of the time. However, once in awhile that did not happen. She might have had an especially trying day and didn't feel very affectionate, or she might have been in a hurry to get to an early evening meeting, or she might have been concentrating on something and didn't want an interruption at exactly that point. Because of any one of these reasons, she might not have responded positively to my show of affection. My prediction would have been wrong that time and I needed to adjust my subsequent communication behavior. Nevertheless, I had predicted a particular response. "Whenever we deliberately communicate with someone, there are certain predictions being made."

Shapiro's third generalization is "People intentionally communicate that in which they feel safe in communicating." I am personally uncomfortable with this statement, and would much prefer "People intentionally communicate that in which they feel *safest* in communicating." It seems to me that there are situations in which no message is "safe," that whatever is said will hurt someone or be interpreted negatively. In these situations, the person will naturally choose to communicate whatever is perceived at the moment to be *least harmful* to the relationship, the other person, or particularly to the communicator's self-image.

This observation of human behavior is usually the unspoken basis for lying. When we perceive that some harm will be done if we tell the truth, or more harm than if we tell a "little white lie," we will tell the lie. We will intentionally communicate that which we perceive as being safest at the time. However, we should be careful not to define "safe" in physical terms only. We human beings need psychological, emotional, and spiritual safety as well, each of which contributes to what we label as our "value system." I illustrated this point to my students with the following story. Back in the early sixties I was an outspoken proponent of the civil rights movement, and, as a citizen of a big city suburb, I was locally involved in its application to fair housing—so much so that it was a frequent topic of conversation around our dinner table. Our two elementary school sons, as children very frequently do, absorbed their parents' point of view.

One warm spring Saturday afternoon, as I was sitting in the living room reading the newspaper, the door flung open and in ran my oldest son, Keith, clothes torn, nose all bloody, tears running down his cheeks. As he made a beeline for the bathroom, I jumped up and, as a deeply concerned father, asked what had happened, to which Keith answered with a very curt "Nuthin," a young boy's way of saying "I don't want to tell you, Dad." Since he didn't seem to be too badly hurt, beyond looking a mess, I overtly respected his privacy. However, I was very curious as to what had happened, so I asked his younger brother. Dean's response was "I'm not going to tell; Keith would kill me!" (His *safest* response!) I then made a deal with Dean: I would not tell Keith that I knew what had happened; it would be a secret between us (a promise I kept until after Keith was out of college). It seems that a group of neighborhood boys was playing cops and robbers in the backyard and a much bigger boy had drawn a bead on Keith after which he said, "Gotcha, ya dirty nigger!" An incensed Keith, fully a head shorter than his "killer," replied with "You don't say that in our yard!" Since no self-respecting bully would let a smaller boy reprimand him without a fight, he came back with "Oh, yeah, ya dirty nigger?!" And the fight was on. Probably Keith

11

didn't even land a blow; Dean didn't know. Why did Keith intentionally communicate to the much larger boy his disapproval of the word "nigger?" He was smart enough to know that it could well bring a physical pounding; and it did. Does this illustration deny the truth of Shapiro's generalization that "People intentionally communicate that in which they feel safe(st) in communicating?"

After a rather long silence, then a number of guesses, some student usually suggested something about conscience, or values. And that is correct. In that brief moment Keith had in which to react to a word he believed obscene, he weighed the consequences and chose the safest path. He would endure the chance of physical abuse rather than the longer lasting hurt from allowing something to be said which ran counter to his values. It would probably hurt him more *not* to register disapproval. Neither path was *safe*, but one was safer than the other in his immediate perception. This seems a rather complex rational process for a fourth grade boy to go through; however, according to Shapiro, it has little to do with maturity. It is only natural communication behavior, something we all do at whatever stage of life, in all probability tied closely to survival needs.

Every week a preacher must make a similar decision during the preparation of the sermon, particularly when some political or social issue is prominant in the news. Do I refer, even obliquely, to that potentially disruptive issue? What is "safest" for me and my vision of the prophetic ministry, for the church fellowship, for my continuing relationship to this congregation? What will be "least costly" in the short run, in the long run? "People (and that includes children and pastors) intentionally communicate that in which they feel safe(st) in communicating."

It might be helpful here to look at the entire process of communicating with the help of a model. There are many from which to choose, models which have been devised by communication scholars over the years. There are mechanistic models, interactive models, transactional models, verbal models, and all kinds of other jargonistic and diagrammatic descriptions of what happens in a communication relationship. Each has its purpose and provides some important and often unique contributions to the understanding of what most of us take for granted. I present here only one model in an attempt both to simplify the explanation and to avoid undue confusion. Following is a representation of communication as developed by William Howell, a model which has made considerable sense to me since I first encountered it in graduate school (lately reprinted in <u>Interpersonal Communication in the Modern Organization</u> by Bormann, Howell, Nichols, and Shapiro).

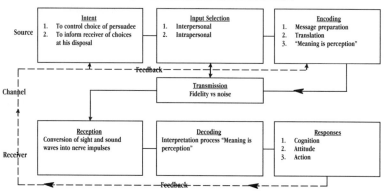

A Universe of Ever-Changing Things, Events, and People

Intent	Input Selection	Encoding
Source 1. To control choice of persuadee 2. To inform receiver of choices at his disposal	1. Interpersonal 2. Intrapersonal	1. Message preparation 2. Translation 3. "Meaning is perception"

Feedback

Channel

Transmission
Fidelity vs noise

Reception	Decoding	Responses
Receiver Conversion of sight and sound waves into nerve impulses	Interpretation process "Meaning is perception"	1. Cognition 2. Attitude 3. Action

Feedback

In order to understand how we can make use of such a model, I want to apply it to a common pastoral situation: calling on a new family in the area. The visiting pastor probably would have as an *intent* to invite the family to worship with the congregation next Sunday, with the eventual goal of becoming members. That intent can be accompanied by one of two underlying motives: 1) to control the family's choice by stressing why and how the pastor's church is superior to any other church in the community; or 2) to inform the family of the choices available in the community, the pastor's church among them. After establishing the intent, the pastor would gather and organize as many reasons (*input* selection) as deemed necessary to fulfill whichever intent/motive was chosen. These bits of information are selected from the pastor's experience, from interpersonal relationships and/or from thoughts and ideas generated from the pastor's perception of the needs of the moment. Once the ideas are selected, the pastor then chooses the words (*encoding*) and the nonverbal accompaniments to be the vehicles for the intended message.

With the words selected to convey the meaning intended, the pastor uses his/her voice to talk—to move the air over the larynx in a patterned way and disturb the atmosphere around the body sufficiently to cause sound waves which can be heard by another person—a behavior that is natural to most living beings, and certainly to most human beings (*transmission*). This transmission process occurs with many possible levels of fidelity, depending upon the amount of external noise in the room (television running, people talking in other rooms, kids dashing through the house, clock ticking, phone ringing, etc.), and internal noise within each person in the conversation (pressures of time, level of irritability, reaction to the temperature in the room, memories, guilt feelings, repressed emotions, etc.). The more noise occurring, the more chance of communication distortion.

The prospective member of the church then receives the sound (*reception*) when the disturbed air causes the ear drum to quiver which, in turn, is converted into nerve impulses to the brain (and, simultaneously, the eye receives the nonverbal message which is similarly transmitted to the

15

brain). This phase of the process is totally physical and is limited only by physical or psychophysical disability. Only after such physical reception of the message(s) does the brain begin the *decoding* phase; that is, translating the sights and sounds into meaningful messages—of course, meaningful according to the *receiver's* own experience and perception. This is very much an interpretive phase of the process. Then, after meaning has been accorded the bits of sight and sound, some kind of reaction takes place (*response*). This could be in the realm of the intellect, the emotions, the physical behavior, or any combination of the three. The response may be positive, negative, or neutral. It may be observable or not.

This response, or seeming lack of it, becomes *feedback* to the pastor, who, upon receiving and interpreting it, then has the opportunity to alter the intent, the input, the encoding, or even the transmission in order to send a more acceptable and effective message. If, for instance, the pastor reads the prospect's response as being hostile for some reason (e.g., because of a feeling of being pressured), the intent might be changed from trying to control choice to one of informing the person of the many choices of churches available in the community. Or, if the response is interpreted as confusion about an idea or suggested activity, the pastor can select another example or explanation (input) which might be more persuasive. Or, if the response is perceived as a problem with a word or phrase, the pastor can choose another expression to convey the idea (encoding). Maybe there's a concern over the "noise" during the conversation, either external or internal (transmission). The pastor can suggest they turn off the television set or even meet some other time or place to discuss the purpose of the visit. This feedback, or interpretation of the perceived response (as indicated by the dotted line in Figure 1), is a critical part of the whole communication process. Accuracy in communicating is determined in large part through an effective use of feedback; that is, interpreting responses and selecting appropriate counter-responses.

The conversants, of course, are interacting without being consciously aware of the process steps; they are doing this naturally, conscious of the content, rarely of the process. Another point worth considering is the fact that this whole process can occur in as short a time as a microsecond. From intent to encoding, from reception to response, during the blinking of an eye. Add to all this the awareness that even as the pastor is sending messages to the prospective communicant and interpreting responses and choosing counter-responses, the prospective member is sending messages to the pastor and interpreting responses and choosing counter-responses. This is happening simultaneously, even though they might be taking turns actually talking. A further complication to this whole process is that it takes place in "a universe of ever-changing things, events, and people." There is no "going back" and redoing a conversation. The two people could start another conversation, but they cannot return to the former moment and relive it. Time has elapsed. They are different people than they were even just a few seconds ago. Their environment has changed. They have had an effect on each other, an effect that was not present at the beginning of the original conversation. To return to Shapiro's fourth generalization on communication: with all its complexities and possibilities for problems to occur, it is no wonder "the *normal* result of the communicating process is at least partial *mis*understanding!"

Much more could be said about communication theory as a background to understanding human interaction; however, these few basics will suffice as a springboard for discussion of the selected topics in succeeding chapters. If a pastor will raise her/his awareness of these communication basics, some sense will emerge from much of the confusing "babble" around us.

Chapter Two
Who Am I?

"Now the word of the Lord came to me saying, 'Before I formed you in the womb I knew you, and before you were born I consecrated you; I appointed you a prophet to the nations.' Then I said, 'Ah, Lord God! Truly I do not know how to speak, for I am only a boy.' But the Lord said to me, 'Do not say, "I am only a boy"; for you shall go to all to whom I send you, and you shall speak whatever I command you. Do not be afraid of them, for I am with you to deliver you, says the Lord.'"
Jeremiah 1:4-8 NRSV

"I am only a boy!" How telling! Of course, this may have been only an excuse for remaining silent. However, I am inclined to believe this was more of a fundamental self-perception Jeremiah held, a self-image which would determine whatever he would attempt or avoid in life. "I am only a boy;" I'm limited; I can't.

Self-concept is where communication begins. Many years ago, when a colleague and I were becoming acquainted, we were sharing, over lunch, what we were teaching that term. I named the four courses I had been assigned to teach, then it was his turn. With a broad smile he said, "I'm teaching Chuck Vick I, Chuck Vick II, Chuck Vick III, and

Chuck Vick IV." We laughed about that, and readily agreed that was probably more true than not for all of us. Regardless of the content of our ideas or the sound of our voices, when we get right down to it, first and foremost we communicate ourselves. This is no less true for pastors than it is for teachers, or any other human being.

Many a pastor, being caught up in "God-talk," becomes so message-centered that s/he forgets that this message comes clothed in the pastor's person— at least in the perception of the hearer. This is not to deprecate the power of the Holy Spirit in the message itself; rather, it is to acknowledge the findings of communication studies, and maybe even the power of the Holy Spirit in the perception of the people of God. The personhood, or personality, of the message-sender is the vehicle bearing the message, and the person's self-concept is seldom completely hidden from the receiver—at least for any extended period of time. (Could this be the basis for the saying attributed to Abraham Lincoln?— "You can fool all of the people some of the time, and some of the people all of the time, but not all of the people all of the time.") It behooves any person with an important message to share (such as the Gospel) to understand this connection of message and person, and that we do indeed, to a great extent, communicate ourselves in the very core of the message we speak. Therefore, it is wise for any person to ponder seriously just who is this self who is communicating.

"Who am I?" "I am only a boy," said Jeremiah. Unless and until the Lord adjusted the young man's thinking with a gentle but firm reprimand, Jeremiah would have communicated in a self-deprecating style, and most certainly would have diminished his power of influence by inviting responses such as "Of course, he's only a boy. . ."

"Who am I?" If I don't know, or haven't thought seriously about it, I will be in the dark as to a goodly part of my message, for who I am will be defined and interpreted *entirely* by my listeners. I will have given complete control of this part of the message over to them. However, if I'm willing to do some introspection and figure out how I really see myself and how well I like myself, I then can use this information to assist in understanding my audience's perception of me and my message, and make any necessary adjustments to enhance my effectiveness. I must be careful, though, not to expect my audience to see me exactly as I see myself. They will be seeing me with their own perceptual powers and according to their experience with similar behaviors and events. During the communication interaction we will be adjusting both self-concept and perceptions of it. (More on this in succeeding chapters.)

On numerous occasions I exhibit a behavior which is discomforting to others: I speak very deliberately and with strong syllabic emphasis. To these others I may sound very certain of myself, very pedantic, and even overbearing. If I were not aware that this behavior was rooted in my self-concept, I probably would be confused by and not alert to both the verbal and nonverbal reaction to this style of speaking, and would not make occasional reference to this behavior and the defensive reaction it sometimes receives. Part of my self-concept is a person who struggles to be understood, certainly reinforced now by Shapiro's fourth generalization. In an effort to be understood, to decrease the misunderstanding natural to all communication, sometimes I speak very deliberately, emphasizing particular syllables, especially on issues important to me. This is frequently received as certainty, and to some people, certainty is perceived as an overbearing attempt at persuasion. Occasionally, during the interchange of ideas, I will notice in the other person confusion, anger, or defensiveness. I am now sensitive to the probability that this is a reaction to my speaking style of the moment. Because I am more aware today, not only of this behavior, but also of its roots in my self-concept, I can make adjustments in my delivery style or self-disclose as to the reasons I speak this way: that I have a personal need to be understood, not that I'm attempting to cram something down anybody's throat.

From this, and from numerous other illustrations we could generate out of our personal experiences, we can conclude that the self-concept is *not* objective. I may be understood quite well without the deliberative style of speaking; but I don't see myself, for whatever reason, as particularly clear. Our self-concepts are subjective, depending upon our unique perceptions of our own experiences and needs. Truly blessed is the person with *honest* friends who will share their more objective views and help the person to check out the accuracy of her/his self-concept. Doubly blessed is the pastor with such honest friends!

Not only does the pastor communicate out of and through a self-concept, but everybody else in the parish does, too. As pastors, we may talk in the morning with a "self-made man" who has experienced nothing but success in his life and who exudes almost excessive confidence, and in the afternoon we may counsel with a battered woman who believes she deserves the physical abuse she's receiving, and in the evening meet with a young person unsure of the future and afraid to leave the security of home and hometown. All different self-concepts, and each with a corresponding level of self-confidence, and each a major determinant of the message being sent.

As pastors we need to understand the important part self-concept (ours and others') plays in our vocational communication, to identify our own self-concept and check out how it corresponds with how others see us, to identify self-image problems in those who come to us for help, and to know how to raise these self-images to a more satisfying and productive level.

First, let's look at the part self-concept plays in communication. Recall a time you had a bad case of the "uglies," when you felt very "down on yourself," when something very important to you failed to make it through your administrative board partly because of something you either said or didn't say, when you were faced with conducting an unexpected funeral and the sermon wasn't done for Sunday and your family had scheduled an outing and you had to disappoint them. How well did you communicate under the pressure of mounting personal inadequacy? Probably not very happily, or effectively. Your own self-concept of the moment was affecting your communication. It is currently popular to lump such pressure-situations under the umbrella term "stress," so the tendency is to look outside of yourself at some kind of stress management seminar or workshop for help. However, you may be able to handle the situation as well by yourself by analyzing and adjusting your self-image.

Now think back to a time when all was going extraordinarily well. Everything important you did turned out successfully. You could even "fall into the river and come out with a new suit!" How did you feel about yourself? Very positive, in all probability; a feeling that affected your communication with others. Your nonverbal behavior and paralanguage (the sounds and silences that carry one's words) betrayed your self-concept. As your communication during that bad case of the "uglies" set the stage for further defeat, so this "top of the world" self-concept tends to bring about further success. Whereas with the "uglies" a minor communication defeat might devestate you, when you're "on top of the world," you can either laugh away a little setback or place it in better perspective. In either case, your self-concept definitely affected the way you communicated with others.

The self-concept (that relatively stable set of perceptions you hold of yourself) begins to develop very early in life. (Some people believe development begins in the womb, and some believe as late as six or seven months, but that's an academic question beyond the scope of this book.) Through the process of experiencing life, the self-concept is reinforced and modified. How one is taught to perceive the world, in combination with genetic tendencies, will determine what experiences are selected to influence the self-concept. The present moment in a person's history is understood through the "eyes" of accumulated experience, particularly the feedback from others, through one's view of physical self, values, roles, talents, emotional states, likes, dislikes, etc., all sorted and selected and applied to the self-concept.

The primary source of messages influencing our self-concept is the family. It is there we are provided with our first feelings of worth, adequacy, and acceptance (or lack of them). These feelings are then reinforced or modified by later experiences, particularly in school and with peers. Later, our record of successes and failures in our vocations and with our intimate relationships influence how we see ourselves and how well we like what we see.

Once the self is fairly well formed, only a powerful force can change it radically. With Jeremiah it was the firm voice of God. As it was with the prophet, the change agent must fulfill at least four basic requirements to be effective. The force must be someone who is seen as competent to influence. Second, the appraisal must be perceived as highly personal. Third, it must be reasonable in light of what we believe about ourselves and of the values we hold. Lastly, it must be consistently reinforced, at least until it becomes an established part of the self-concept. The Lord God was perceived by Jeremiah to be very competent, the message was highly personal, it was reasonable given Jeremiah's understanding of the Faith, and the promise was made for continuing reinforcement of the Lord's presence.

When the son of a single mother participates in the Big Brother program, we often see these four factors working together to raise that boy's self-concept. If matched properly, here is a big brother with some amount of skill in the boy's activity-interest, therefore seen as competent to influence. The regular one-on-one relationship is perceived as highly personal. The reasonableness of the association is not always accepted, especially by a youngster whose level of trust has been beaten low, but when it can be understood as a *mutually* beneficial relationship, this third factor is met. Lastly, this relationship must continue to be reinforced by regular meetings and activities, an indicator of the worth both of the boy and of the big brother relationship. When these four factors exist, a young man's self-concept and self-confidence raises significantly.

The self-concept is multidimensional (Adler, Rosenfeld, & Towne, Interplay, 4th ed.). It is very complex. First is the self as perceived by the self, that view most often constructed around the interpreted feedback others give. The second dimension is the desired self, that view of an idealized image, whether obtainable or not, based primarily on what the person has been taught to think s/he *ought* to be. The third dimension of the self- concept is the presenting self, a view based on the kind of self one is attempting to present through one's behavior; that is, the kind of person I am trying to make you believe I am by the way I'm presenting myself. Still another dimension of the self-concept is its situationality. Oftimes the situation and the immediate relationship determines to a great extent the self-concept with its built-in fluidity. A pastor probably would not hold the same view of self when returning to seminary for a continuing education credit course in systematic theology with a world-reknowned scholar as s/he might have when teaching a Bible study in the local parish. Each of these dimensions, singly and in conjunction with each other, will invariably affect a person's communication with others.

Large segments of society have been drastically affected by the self-concepts dominant within a culture. A few years ago, when I was making this point in an interpersonal communication class I was teaching to a hospital staff, one of the class members shared an article with me (and later with the class) which very aptly illustrates this (Theodora Wells, <u>Newsletter, Association for Humanistic Psychology</u>, December 1970). It is an article heavily steeped in Freudian concepts and terminology, and if this offends the reader, I can only ask that you look beyond Freud to how the described culture would indeed affect the self-concept of both males and females.

> ...The following experience is an invitation to awareness in which you are asked to feel into, and stay with, your feelings through each step, letting them absorb you. If you start intellectualizing, go back to the step where you can again sense your feelings. Then proceed. Keep count of how many times you need to go back.

1. Consider reversing the generic term Man. Think of the future of Woman which, of course, includes both women and men. Feel into that, sense its meaning to you—as a woman—as a man.
2. Think of it always being that way, every day of your life. Feel the ever-presence of woman and feel the non-presence of man. Absorb what it tells you about the importance and value of being woman—of being man.
3. Recall that everything you have ever read all your life uses only female pronouns—she, her—meaning both girls and boys, both women and men. Recall that most of the voices on radio and most of the faces on TV shows are women's—when important events are covered—on commercials—and on late talk shows. Recall that you have one male senator representing you in Washington.
4. Feel into the fact that women are the leaders, the power-centers, the prime-movers. Man, whose natural role is husband and father, fulfills himself through nurturing children and making the home a refuge for woman. This is only natural to balance the biological role of woman who devotes her entire body to the race during pregnancy. Pregnancy—the most revered power known to woman (and man, of course).
5. Then feel further into the obvious biological explanation for woman as the ideal: her genital construction. By design, female genitals are compact and internal, protected by her body. Male genitals are so exposed that he must be protected from outside attack to assure the perpetuation of the race. His vulnerability obviously requires sheltering.
6. Thus, by nature, males are more passive than females, and have a desire in sexual relations to be symbolically engulfed by the protective body of the woman. Males psychologically yearn for this protection, fully realizing their masculinity at this time, and feeling exposed and vulnerable at other times. A man experiences himself as a "whole man" when thus engulfed.
7. If the male denies these feelings, he is unconsciously rejecting his masculinity. Therapy is thus indicated to help him adjust to his own nature. Of course, therapy is administered by a woman, who has the education and wisdom to facilitate openness leading to the male's growth and self-actualization.
8. To help him feel into his defensive emotionality, he is invited to get in touch with the "child" in him. He remembers his sister's jeering at his primitive genitals that "flop around foolishly." She can run, climb, and ride horseback unencumbered. Obviously, since she is free to move, she is encouraged to develop her body and mind

29

in preparation for her active responsibilities of adult womanhood. The male vulnerability needs female protection, so he is taught the less active, caring virtues of homemaking.

9. Because of his vagina-envy, he learns to bind up his genitals, and learns to feel ashamed and unclean because of his nocturnal emissions. Instead, he is encouraged to dream of getting married, waiting for the time of his fulfillment—when "his woman" gives him a girl-child to care for. He knows that if it is a boy-child he has failed somehow—but they can try again.

10. In getting to the "child" in him, these early experiences are reawakened. He is at an encounter group entitled, "On Being a Man" which is led by a woman. In a circle of 19 men and 4 women, he begins to work through some of his deep feelings.

. . .What feelings do *you* think he will express?

When I read this to my Interpersonal Communication classes, I made it part of an involvement exercise. I placed them in groups of four, in each group a mixture of males and females, hopefully two of each. I asked them to listen carefully and to imagine themselves living in the culture being described, yet being the same sex they are now. I further asked them to monitor their feelings and reactions as I read. After the reading, I asked them to share their feelings with each other about being a male or a female in the newly described culture. After they resisted a bit and tried to intellectualize ("That's not the way it is!" "Women don't have it that bad today!" "That could never happen here!"), with a little urging from me, they began to share with each other how living in such a culture would make them feel about themselves. From the males I overheard comments like "I'd feel like shit," and "Completely powerless"

30

and "Very angry!" From the females I overheard "Strong," "Confident," "Important," and "In control." The students began to realize that much of their self-concept is inculturated, the sex of a person being one major influence in its development. So it is with racial and ethnic groups (an excellent example of this is the 1970 educational film by Xerox titled "The Eye of the Storm," the documentary story of Jane Elliot, an innovative third grade teacher in Riceville, Iowa who was trying to teach her culturally ignorant students what discrimination was, and separated the blue-eyed children from those with brown eyes, giving privileges to one group and not to the other, all based on the "obvious" reality that blue-eyed people were better than brown-eyed ones, and later vice-versa, with the result of the lowering and raising of their self-concepts), with the mentally handicapped, with the economically deprived, and with numerous other categories of people. Self-concept being affected by religious affiliation or experience is not unknown either. In some congregations, those who have never experienced being "born again" feel like "second-class citizens." As is the opposite true in some other congregations. Self-concepts rise and fall largely by the perceptive behavior of others, and these self-concepts affect the way we communicate with each other.

I suggest, therefore, that each pastor attempt to identify her/his own self-image, and check it out with others as part of the process of assessing its impact on communication effectiveness. To begin, you might jot down on a sheet of paper answers to the following questions: "How do you see yourself? What image do you believe you project to others? What 'type' of person do they see you to be? Do their typical reactions to you present any consistent pattern which might reveal how they think of you? Try to recall interaction with your parents, relatives, siblings, and peers when you were a child. How do you perceive that you were perceived? What seemed to be expected of you? What connections can you make between your self-image now and roles and behaviors expected of you when you were a child? As a consequence of your total experiences in life thus far, how do you see yourself as a communicator today?" This list of questions was my initial assignment to my interpersonal communication classes whose members were both traditional and nontraditional (adults twenty-five years of age and older) students. Both groups often indicated to me that this was the most difficult "paper" they had ever written, but also among the most helpful.

After this initial jotting, I suggest you move on to another exercise in order to focus more clearly on your self-image. This is an adaptation of a textbook exercise I used regularly.

Below are twelve categories of personal characteristics. Write two specific characteristics that best describe you in the spaces provided.

A. Statements about your talents or creative abilities.
    1. _____
    2. _____

B. Statements about your physical appearance or condition.
    1. _____
    2. _____

C. Statements about your intellectual abilities.
    1. _____
    2. _____

D. Statements about your political beliefs.
    1. _____
    2. _____

E. Statements about your spiritual beliefs.
    1. _____
    2. _____

F. Statements about yourself as a friend.
    1. _____
    2. _____

G. Statements about yourself as a member of your family-of-origin.
    1. _____
    2. _____

H. Statements about yourself as a member of your present family.
    1. _____
    2. _____

I. Statements about yourself as a pastor.
    1. _____
    2. _____

J. Statements about your feelings or moods.
    1. _____
    2. _____

K. Statements about yourself as a communicator.
    1. _____
    2. _____

L. Statements about your goals for your future.
    1. _____
    2. _____

Having meditated on your answers in these two exercises, figuring out what you <u>think</u> about yourself, the next step is to assess how <u>self-accepting</u> you are, given these responses. This is to emphasize that viewing the self is not the same as accepting one's self-worth, that one does not automatically lead to the other. To "get a handle" on how self-accepting you are, I suggest another brief exercise (from Hopper & Whitehead's <u>Communication Concepts and Skills</u>).

Indicate your preferred response to the following statements by circling that response. There are no right or wrong answers. The best answer is the one that applies to you.

__ 1. I do not question my worth as a person, even if I think others do.

1	2	3	4	5
Not at all true of me	Slightly true of me	About half true of me	Mostly true of me	True of me

__ 2. When people say nice things about me, I find it difficult to believe that they really mean it. I think that maybe they are kidding me or just are not being sincere.

1 True	2 MT	3 HT	4 ST	5 Not True

__ 3. * The person you marry may not be perfect, but I believe in trying to get him or her to change along desirable lines.

1 True	2 MT	3 HT	4 ST	5 Not True

__ 4. I look on most of the feelings and impulses I have toward people as being quite natural and acceptable.
   1 Not True   2 ST   3 HT   4 MT   5 True

__ 5.* I usually ignore the feelings of others when I am trying to accomplish some important end.
   1 True   2 MT   3 HT   4 ST   5 Not True

__ 6. I do not say much at social affairs because I am afraid that people will criticize me or laugh if I say the wrong thing.
   1 True   2 MT   3 HT   4 ST   5 Not True

__ 7.* There are very few times when I compliment people for their talents or jobs they have done.
   1 True   2 MT   3 HT   4 ST   5 Not True

__ 8.* I can be friendly with people who do things that I consider wrong.
   1 Not True   2 ST   3 HT   4 MT   5 True

Now write the number you circled for each statement in the blank to the left of it. Add up the numbers for the statements that have an asterisk (*) and write that number here ___ (accepting of others as they are). Add up the numbers for the statements without asterisks and write that number here ___ (self-accepting). Add the two numbers together ___. Consider the nearer you are to 40 as a total, the more self-accepting you are, based on the fairly-well documented premise that the more you accept others as they are, the more self-accepting you tend to be.

Another way to look at your self-concept is to consider how well you *like* yourself (apart from *accepting* yourself). By answering the following statements truthfully you can get a broad idea of how happy you are with yourself. (Exercise reprinted from Adler and Towne's Looking Out, Looking In, 1st ed.)

Next to each statement put a number that reflects your feeling:

    4 if you always feel this way
    3 if you feel this way most of the time
    2 if you feel this way some of the time
    1 if you feel this way only once in awhile
    0 if you never feel this way

1. ____ I enjoy waking up in the morning.
2. ____ I'm usually in a good mood.
3. ____ Most people like me.
4. ____ When I look in a mirror, I like what I see.
5. ____ If I were a member of the opposite sex, I'd find me attractive.
6. ____ I'm intelligent.
7. ____ I enjoy my work.
8. ____ There aren't very many things about myself I'm ashamed of.
9. ____ I feel comfortable about the number of my friendships.
10. ___ I have plenty of energy.
11. ___ I'm basically an optimistic person.
12. ___ I can laugh at my mistakes.
13. ___ If I could live my life over, there isn't much I would change.
14. ___ I'm an interesting person.
15. ___ I'm happy with my sex life.
16. ___ I'm still growing and changing.
17. ___ Other people care about me.
18. ___ There's nobody quite like me.
19. ___ There's not much I would change about my appearance.
20. ___ I'm a kind person.
21. ___ I don't have many regrets about my life.
22. ___ The people I care about value my opinions.
23. ___ I'm not afraid to express my feelings.
24. ___ If there's a heaven, I'll go there after I die.
25. ___ I feel comfortable in a conversation.
26. ___ I can make of my life whatever I want.
27. ___ There aren't very many people I'd trade places with.
28. ___ I've led an interesting life.
29. ___ Nothing is too good for me.
30. ___ I like where I live.

If your total is above 95, congratulations; you have a very positive self-concept. However, if you scored above 108, you may have an inflated ego that might be turning off other people. If your total is 72-95, you are among the lucky people who really like themselves. Everything is not perfect; you see room for improvement, but you have the self-acceptance resources to make those improvements. If your total is 48-71, you have mixed feelings about yourself. You may be concentrating too much on your perceived weaknesses and not enough on your strengths. If your total is 47 or below, you are not very happy with yourself. You may just be having a "bad day," or you may be shortchanging yourself. Do the exercise again in a week, and if your score is this low again, it might be wise to talk to someone you trust and check on how they see you. Not being happy with yourself often "turns off" others with whom you communicate.

Again, how we see ourselves and how well we accept and like what we see will be communicated to others one way or another as the relationship develops. Our self-concepts will have an impact on how and what we communicate, be it from the pulpit, in a committee meeting, or at the cafe over a cup of coffee. The pastor who is aware of her/his own self-concept will be far more effective as a communicator than the counterpart who isn't aware. To know that the self-concept is a major part of the message, and what that self-concept is, is a giant step toward reducing misunderstanding between yourself and others. Being thus aware will allow you an opportunity to adjust your communication to compensate for any problem caused by the "self" part of your message.

As stated earlier, as it is with the pastor, so also is it true with the people we shepherd: their self-concepts affect their communication, too. Their family upbringing and life-experiences also determine how they view themselves and how well they accept and like themselves. The pastor who understands this is a long way toward effectively ministering to their needs. As with us, some of the views they have of themselves are true only because they allow them to be. The view often is unrealistic and definitely counterproductive. Part of a pastor's task, in ministering to their needs, may be to help them recognize this. One way might be to listen for such phrases as "I can't" or frequent self-denigrations. These are clues to a low self-concept. Raising of one's self concept is a way of fulfilling the scriptural admonition: "You shall know the truth and the truth shall set you free;" for a more positive self-concept truly is a freeing acquisition.

Without using this as a formal exercise, a pastor might well make use of something I have found very helpful in the classroom. Whenever a low-self-concept person says "I can't," suggest that s/he might more appropriately say "I won't," *and*, importantly, the person has every right to make that conscious choice which "won't" denotes. This person *does* have control over much of life; that "can't" is often a "cop-out." Yes, there are some things we *can't* do or be, but they are far fewer than we oftimes declare. We are choice-makers, and in general we may do a fairly good job at our choicemaking. We are, however, subject less often than we'd like to admit to the fates of "can't." Of course, reminding a low self-concept person of this truth must be accompanied by a sincere acknowledgment of their worth as an individual choicemaker, of your acceptance of them and of their right to say "I won't," rather than the more self-deprecating "I can't."

When interacting with people who are regularly "putting themselves down," a ministry to them might be reminding them of their strengths, and suggesting they spend some moments in "self-appreciation." Most of us in this culture grew up with the admonition not to "brag." Over the years this has been translated into "Don't say anything good about yourself." How unfortunate! Since everyone needs some positive strokes, we have developed a society of "manipulators" who often structure conversations so the other person will give them a compliment. "What do you think of my newly decorated living room?" instead of "I like how I decorated my living room; do you like it?" In all probability, the decorator likes the result, so why not give the self a compliment? Sadly, if this person were to comment on her/his decorating talents, s/he would say something like "I'm not a very good decorator, but I did my best," thus leading the other person to say something positive about the new look and the decorator's talents. If I can't (won't?) say something good about myself, I need to get you to say it for me.

There are some people in our parishes, hopefully very few, who seldom hear anything positive about themselves. I am reminded of a film shown frequently to educators by the title "Cipher In The

Snow" (BYU 1970, based on a true story by Jean Mizer in Today's Education, Nov.,1964). It is the story of a boy named Cliff, who one day asked the school bus driver to stop and let him off, only to drop dead in a snow bank once off the bus. Cliff's favorite teacher, who hardly knew the boy, is asked to write an obituary for the school paper. It seems that Cliff was a "zero," a "cipher," a person very few people, adults as well as children, even knew. As flashbacks are shown, it becomes obvious that Cliff was a person who received little or no positive feedback, a young man to whom only negative comments were made, a young man who finally just gave up and died. Before his world had come crashing in on him, Cliff seemed to be a normal child with an average IQ and curiosity about the world. Then a number of circumstances and events occurred which devastated his self-image, and, like that well known illustration of those babies in the hospital without any physical attention beyond feeding and changing, Cliff just "rolled over, turned his face to the wall, and died." Some people in our parishes, from lack of any positive attention, are dying, too. Their self-image, self-concept, self-esteem needs some constructive attention. It is part of our ministry, just as much as it was part of Jesus' ministry when he gave some attention to the woman at the well, communicating to her that she was important to him. Zaccheus and others felt the same confirmation of worth through Jesus' attention, and they were never the same because of it. We do have the power to affect change in the self-concept of other people.

Adler and Towne, again in the first edition of their popular Interpersonal Communication textbook, <u>Looking Out, Looking In</u>, tell the story of Margaret, a quiet, withdrawn coed with a definite self-image problem. Two male classmates take it upon themselves to "try an experiment" and see how true it is that some positive attention could really change a personality. They talk with her, ask her opinion about their courses, listen to her, and eventually ask her for a date. Their attention influences Margaret to dress differently, walk more confidently, fix her hair more attractively, even offer an opinion in class without being called upon. The young man telling the story looks forward to his turn to date Margaret; however, whenever his asks, she is always busy with other dates, she being more popular now with her new self-image. The storyteller ends by admitting that the "experiment worked," but that his self-image is now shaken a bit. I am *not* recommending that anyone attempt "experimenting" on another human being, as these two young men did with Margaret. I *am* suggesting that we can, by paying positive attention to people, by complimenting them, by focusing on their strengths, create an environment in which they will see themselves more positively, thus raising their self-concept. This, in turn, will enhance their communication skills, and thereby affect everybody who interacts with them.

One evening my wife, LuBell, and I were grocery shopping in a local supermarket. She was wearing a sweatshirt with the name and logo of our local university emblazoned on the front. Suddenly, a college-age young man, a stranger, wearing a warm smile and standing next to LuBell, a gray-haired fifty-plus lady, said to her, "I like your sweatshirt; you could easily be elected Homecoming Queen at the University." Without waiting for a response, he then just walked away down the aisle. LuBell immediately thought that was one of my students just trying to be funny. When I assured her that I didn't know the young man (and I didn't), an inner glow began to emerge within her. She was attractive to this young man, and the compliment seemed spontaneously and freely given with no thought of any kind of reward, other than the giving of it. LuBell has no problem with her self-concept any more than any other normal human being; however, the memory of that one compliment stayed with her for at least a couple of weeks, helping her to feel better about herself. If such a comment can have such a positive and lasting effect on a strong person, imagine how great an impact one compliment can have on a low self-concept person who really hungers for someone to say something nice about her/him!

Another learning exercise we did in class was

called "Uppers and Downers," again one designed by Adler and Towne. In this experience we recall, in small discussion or sharing groups, particular instances in which 1) we influenced someone to feel better about themselves by what we said to them, 2) we influenced someone to feel worse about themselves because of our words, 3) someone influenced us to feel better about ourselves by what they said to us, and 4) someone influenced us to feel worse about ourselves because of their words. The goal of this exercise was to show that our words do have an effect on another's self-concept: an "upper" makes us feel better about ourselves, and a "downer" makes us feel worse about ourselves. As pastors, we need to remember this, particularly since our opinion (perception) is often taken more seriously than we sometimes think. Some people receive more "downers" then they need, even on a daily basis, and could use an occasional "upper" from their pastor.

A final word on self-concept. As pastors, we need to be careful not to promulgate "the myth of perfection." This is an all-too-common belief in the perfectability of human behavior, a belief that seems to have its roots in the parental encouragement of their children to excel at whatever they do, to come out number one, to feel somewhat ashamed of being less than the very best. With the weight of such a myth bearing on one's shoulders, anything less than perfection in one's behavior and

43

accomplishments will be noted, if not by someone else, then by the inner self. Guilt occurs; self-concept is diminished; communication skills suffer; relationships are adversely affected. It was an odd sight one year at the conclusion of the award ceremony at the Minnesota High School state basketball tournament when the second place team, which had just been beaten by the new state champions, raced around the court grinning and raising their arms with two fingers extended. They were number two in the state and were proud of it. Contrast that scene with the "normal" one of tears pouring forth from the beaten, unsuccessful finalists. That coach and those young men are to be congratulated, for they were striking a blow at "the myth of perfection," an unfortunate standard that does little else than erode a positive self-concept in all of us.

Chapter Three
Through the Eyes of the Beholder

"Now when Jesus came into the district of Caesarea Philippi, he asked his disciples, 'Who do people say that the Son of Man is?' And they said, 'Some say John the Baptist, but others Elijah, and still others Jeremiah or one of the prophets.' He said to them, 'But who do you say that I am?' Simon Peter answered, 'You are the Messiah, the Son of the living God.'"

Matthew 16:13-16 NRSV

Simon Peter saw through the eyes of Faith what others without those eyes did not see. He perceived Jesus differently than they did. Jesus was the same person; only the perceivers' experiences with Jesus differed. Not that perception creates universal reality, rather an individual's perception creates reality for the perceiver.

This is important for the pastor to understand. One's background of accumulated experiences is an active filter to everything a person senses, to every idea with which a person is confronted, to every emotion expressed, to every desire felt, and to every act committed. In a very real sense, our reality is determined by the tapestry scene we have woven with the threads of our daily experiences, and against which all that we observe in ourselves and in others is played, compared, contrasted, and understood. Why did Simon Peter see Jesus as the Christ when many others did not? Because his past experiences, his hopes, dreams, and expectations, especially those of the recent past, wove his tapestry scene in which he would live the rest of his life, and according to which he would interpret and understand whatever would happen in the future.

That the answer to a social problem is clear to the pastor does not mean it is clear to everyone or even a majority in the parish. Any church body not satisfied with the status quo knows how true this is! Administrative boards and parish councils have been split asunder over differing perceptions. Equally committed people can hold opposite views, and often do. Is it merely a matter of someone being obstinate, or self-serving, or "in league with the devil?" That may be true once in a while, but usually not, as much as we'd like to think it was that simple. The threads of their past experiences have woven a different tapestry, a different world against which they view the contemporary issue.

When the pastor is aware of this phenomenon, opposition is often less of a problem to understand. Instead of trying to solve the problems of two different worlds, instead of expending energy uselessly head to head in unending conflict, the pastor can put time and energy into providing experiences which might alter the other person's worldview. During the heyday of the civil rights struggles in the 1960's, when involved in the aforementioned suburban tension, I learned through one unfortunate experience after another that open confrontation over this moral issue was more counterproductive than I wished it would be. Only when I provided voluntary experiences of interracial contact, coupled with less-impassioned reasoning, did I even begin to make headway. These "experience-threads" created a different tapestry for many of my parishoners—a different world than they had seen before having these experiences. Now that they had a glimpse of the same world in which I operated, there was an opportunity to work together on a more compatible solution to the problem. Of course, in this whole process, I glimpsed the world which they saw and was able to understand them and their needs better, thereby potentially being a more effective pastor to them.

There are so many facets of perception that bear upon the communicating process it is difficult to know how much to include in a single chapter. Whole courses in college and continuing education weekend seminars are built around the subject! Much of it seems little else than plain common sense! However, like self-concept, an understanding of the basics of human perception is crucial to an understanding of the communicating process; thus, more needs to be

47

said as a foundation for the ensuing chapters.

Each term in my classes, as I introduced the subject of perception, I had a number of exercises which highlighted the fact that we human beings not only perceive differently, but we also perceive according to our past experiences with like stimula. One very effective exercise was to write two lists on the board, one labeled "unpleasant" and the other labeled "pleasant." The students then called out tastes they considered unpleasant, and I recorded them: jalapeno peppers, warm beer, potato soup, broccoli, liver, etc. Then they called out tastes they considered pleasant, and I recorded them, too: steak, cold beer, coffee, spaghetti; and sometimes I heard: broccoli, jalapeno peppers, warm beer (from a visiting British Islander!), and even liver! Then two lists of odors. Unpleasant: skunk, strong perfume, body odor, hog manure, dirty diapers, diesel exhaust, etc. Pleasant: newly mown hay, after a spring rain, perfume, hog manure (smells like money to the hog farmer!), dirty diapers (relief to parents after a child's feverish bout with constipation!), diesel exhaust (one student's reminder of his high school graduation gift from his parents which was an unlimited Greyhound pass to travel the United States for an entire summer, an experience he remembered with warm memories!). The same points can be made comparing pleasant and unpleasant lists of sounds, touches, and scenes: we perceive differently, based both on our genetic abilities and limitations and on the past experiences we've had and which we associate with the stimula. This becomes part of our connotative meaning.

A parish example of visual perception might be relevant here. For many years I wanted to grow a beard, so one summer vacation (a whole month out of the public eye!) I grew one. Returning to the pulpit on Labor Day Sunday, believing it would be a small congregation anyway that day, I decided not to shave it off. After the service, when shaking hands on the way out of church, one woman who had always supported whatever I suggested, a woman to whom I could always go for encouragement and advice, looked me in the eye with a most determined and angry expression, and said "You'd better shave that off before next Sunday! You look like a damned hippie!" I gulped and smiled sheepishly. A few moments later in the line of greeters was a woman who had been a thorn in my side since I had arrived in that church. I thought to myself, "If my beard got that kind of reaction from a friend, what will this person say?" When she was directly in front of me, I extended my hand and as I looked at her I noticed she had a tear in her eye and the most benevolent expression I had ever seen on her face. She very softly said, "I'll never oppose you again in your ministry here." During that brief moment between sentences, I remember thinking "She's been converted! Praise the Lord!" Then she continued, "When you stood up there in the pulpit wearing that beard, all I could think of was my pastor when I was a little girl. He had a beard just like yours! Thank you." And she gave me a hug! Meaning is perception. Her church-world had changed. I was the same person, but she saw me differently. Her communication behavior with me altered significantly from that day forward.

Perception is involved in so much of our pastoral communication! I remember one couple I counseled on more than one occasion. As young adults they came to me "in love," and wanted to get married. During the pre-marital counseling, as is my custom, I gave each a blank sheet of paper and asked them to write down ten things they liked about the other. They had no trouble doing this, finishing in only a minute or so. Then I asked them to write down five things they did not like about the other. They just stared blankly at me. When I insisted, they reluctantly wrote down a couple of behaviors, but they were struggling. I waited. It was fully fifteen minutes before they completed this list, and then only with constant pressure from me. A few years later, this same couple came to me as a marriage in trouble. They were now looking at divorce, since they were no longer "in love." This time I asked them to write down ten things they did not like about the other person, a task they completed very quickly. And a list of five things they liked about the other, a list they had great difficulty in completing. I waited. Finally, what seemed like ages to them, they finished their list. I then asked them to recall the initial pre-marital interview a few years back, and shared with them that they were relatively the same persons, only that their experiences since that time had altered their perceptions. Until they would reweave positive experiences into the fabric of their world, their marriage would continue to be in trouble. Only when they would concentrate more on their likes than on their dislikes, as they did during their courtship, would their marriage improve. We had discussed the phenomenon of perception, particularly the "halo effect," their expectations as to the level of further interaction. When the couple looked ahead and saw years of married bliss, they looked for only the good things in each other because that's what they wished for and that's what their desired world required. When that same couple looked ahead and saw the end of their relationship, they looked for only the bad things in each other to justify a worldview in which the other person would be absent; they must make their world a better world without the other person in it, and that required remembering only the bad things about the partner.

Examples abound in which a viewer can see in the same photograph or drawing a particular figure or picture one moment and a different figure or picture the next moment, jumping back and forth by concentrating on certain parts of the photo or drawing. Probably the best known is the "old woman/young woman" drawing; others that come to mind are the Eskimo/Indian drawing, the female figure/stairwell spindle picture, the vase/two faces image, and the empty socketed skull/woman at the mirror picture, three of which are pictured below:

A picture more relevant to the purposes of this book, and especially to the above example involving the young couple, is M.C. Escher's drawing of angels and devils. When we concentrate on the angels (the good), the devils (the bad) fade into the background. When we concentrate on the devils, the angels fade into the background. The focus of our energy determines to a great extent what we see—on paper and in other people.

Sometimes, because of genetic or physical limitations or because of inculturation or because

of undeveloped associative powers, a person simply does not/will not see what others see, or does not/ will not hear what others hear.   In our Speech Communication department we had an "illusion machine" which spins black and white patterned disks at varying speeds. We gathered the students at one end of the room with the spinning disks at the other end and asked the students to call out what they saw. "I see bright purple," said one; another said, "Red and shiny brown, sort of alternating;" still another, "Rust with flecks of green." Invariably there'd be at least one person in the group who looked very baffled, almost as if the others were crazy, or that there was a class conspiracy against her/him. Upon urging, the mystified ones would respond with "I see black and white. That's all." Then the others, who were seeing all sorts of pretty colors come and go, tried to show the "black and white" people where the colors were—but to no avail. They simply saw differently.

One instructor took the illusion machine home to show his family and have a bit of fun playing with it. When his wife and his eight-year-old daughter watched it, a very interesting thing happened. His daughter oo'ed and ah'ed over the kaleidoscope of colors she saw, while his wife, known to be a very logical and analytical person, became increasingly irritated at the whole experience, frequently interrupting her daughter's oo'ing and ah'ing with "It's black and white, dear! There are no colors! There's black and white; that's all!" The daughter became increasingly subdued, and began to question her own eyes, similar to those "black and white viewers" in class. Whereas the classroom students, in not seeing what some others were seeing, could understand the concept of individual perception, the mother-daughter relationship, being based on love, respect, and power, was quite another matter. The daughter had a choice: she could go on believing she was seeing pretty colors and thereby be "wrong" in her mother's eyes, or she could convince herself that she really didn't see the colors because mother said they weren't there. In reflecting on her behavior during that "confrontation of perception," the mother later apologized to the daughter and expressed to her that it was really "OK" for them to see differently, for the daughter to see changing colors and for the mother to see only black and white on the spinning disk. This took great courage on the part of that mother, and it was a lasting lesson for both.

This phenomenon extends beyond the physical ability to see. A person's thinking style can define what we value in life; it can determine our priorities; it becomes a perceptual lens through which we see the world. In our dominant culture we have convinced ourselves of the superiority of the mind over the emotions, the mind being the home base of logic, and the emotions being the home of sensory reactions and responses. This perceptual inculturation had tragic results with one young couple I knew. They were very much "in love," and seemingly were well matched in interests, activities, needs, and life goals. He was a person who saw life from a logical point of view; everything he did was systematic, obviously connected, well-reasoned. She, on the other hand, was a person who behaved spontaneously, impulsively, and intuitively. They complemented each other very well. However, he believed that his way was superior to hers, and in their common decisions she should defer to reason. If she had believed as strongly in her perception of how to cope with the world, I think they would have had a successful, though frequently fiery, relationship. However, she had been taught (inculturated) to believe that logic and reason were superior, too. She accepted that, and tried to change. She couldn't, and felt guilty for not "growing up," for not being as "mature" as her husband. She felt inferior, and he agreed. Divorce resulted, and primarily because of a common cultural perception that is not accepted in many parts of the world—that logical thinking is superior to the intuitive.

It is not at all unusual for guilt feelings to spring from perceptual differences, especially in matters of religious faith. This realization was reinforced one day when I showed one of those "what-do-you-see?" pictures to someone. The picture had been given to me by a student in the first course I had ever taught in a university, back in 1968. After a class period in which we had been discussing the subject of perception, he gave me the following photograph, with this explanation. A professional photographer was feeling "out of sorts" one day, not very positive about himself, anxious and apprehensive about life, spiritually and emotionally "down." It had been a long winter. Snow was piled up. Patches of ice made both driving and walking treacherous, yet he needed to get out of his studio since the four walls were closing in on him. So he put on his coat, slung his camera over his shoulder, and set out to take some pictures of the brisk winter day. Maybe that would make him feel better. He snapped pictures of trees heavy with snow, of newly shoveled driveways, of a birdhouse capped with a crown of white. Although taking pictures had always helped him through his moods in the past, nothing this day seemed to remove his depression. Suddenly, his foot struck a patch of ice, he lost his balance, and down he went. As he was falling, his finger inadvertantly squeezed the shutter; it clicked; and he wasted a picture. He stood up, looked around embarrassedly to see if anyone had seen him fall, and proceeded on with his photographic tour, feeling no better when he returned than when he left. He went into his darkroom to develop his roll of film. When he came to the wasted picture he had snapped when he was falling on that patch of ice, he stared in fascination at the emerging image. As he looked at this "snowbank in shadows," he saw something there that was the "answer" to what he had been looking for, that which would remove his sense of depression. At this point in his explanation the student paused and asked me, "What do you think he saw?"

It took me a few moments to organize my perception in such a way as to see a picture of a bearded man in the upper part of the photo. To me, it looked very much like a partial view of Hoffman's "Head of Christ." Yes, confided the young student, that is what the photographer had seen, and, as the story goes, he was never the same after that, a new sense of purpose entered his life, his depression left, and a Christian was either respiritualized or reborn. Over the years I have shown that photograph to numerous classes with the explanation given to me by my student, and it has never ceased to intrigue. (I have since heard other explanations for that particular photograph, but have concluded, from my own informal research, that the one given above is the original.)

This picture and story was connected to guilt feelings by an experience I had a number of years ago. I had an occasion to show this photograph and tell the story to a woman I hold in high regard for the strength of her Christian Faith, her dedication, and her piety. She looked at the picture and saw nothing. She stared at it, turned it upside down, around and around, and finally came up with "A rabbit?" When I told her what the photographer had seen, she still couldn't see the head of Christ, even when I meticulously pointed it out. As we discussed this, she became more and more depressed. What was going through her head? She was thinking, "If I consider myself a Christian, yet cannot see the face of my Master in the picture as many other people do, there must be something wrong with me and my faith." Guilt had entered the picture: she couldn't see, somehow her associative powers and past experiences weren't organizing "properly," what other Christians were seeing, especially the face of Christ, the very cornerstone of their Faith. If she couldn't see something as important as this in a simple photograph, then she wasn't a very good Christian person, so she reasoned. The more she would try to see this "Christ in the Snows," the more frustrated, depressed, and guilty she felt.

Sometimes when we pastors see things our people do not—in pictures, in symbols, in a Scriptural text, in a relationship, in any aspect of faith—we lay groundwork for guilt feelings to emerge. Something must be wrong with them, they sometimes reason, if they do not see things exactly as we, who are considered "experts" in the Faith, see them. The stronger may go to another church to find a pastor who sees the Faith as they do, church-hopping until they find one. The weaker in the Faith may sit there Sunday after Sunday feeling more and more depressed and guilty, or maybe just forget the Church altogether, drop out, nurture their guilt, harbor animosity, and rationalize their absence. We must be aware of perceptual differences in our congregations, and we would be wise to acknowledge them and to make allowances for them, accepting those we can accept as understandable differences. If we cannot "accept" a perception because it seems "way out of line" with the Christian gospel, we can attempt to provide experiences with which such persons might restructure their world. This is certainly a legitimate expression of the teaching aspect of ministry.

Individual perceptions have a habit of reinforcing each other and becoming cultural perceptions. Then we are into stereotyping, which is occasionally helpful in communication, but most often problematical. An example of the more positive use of stereotyping is our rules for safety, especially for children in our society. Many of these common and acceptable rules are based on stereotyping, on cultural perceptions. "Don't speak to strangers." "If a man stops you on the street and offers you candy, run to the nearest policeman and tell him." "If you are home alone and the phone rings, don't tell the voice on the other end that you are alone." We are teaching our children that strangers will hurt them, that policemen will protect them, that voices on the phone are trying to find out if children are alone so they can come and hurt them. As untrue as these are as blanket statements, we still use such stereotyping in an attempt to protect our children.

Cultural perceptions become more of a problem when we adults use them in a prejudicial way. For far too many years, the cultural perception of blacks held by some whites in our nation included characteristics such as naturally musical, commonly lazy and shiftless, difficult to educate, genetically unable to speak distinctly, sexually promiscuous, etc. The movies of yesteryear speak eloquently to this. Oh, we would meet exceptions to this stereotyped image, but that's what they were considered: exceptions. In general, all blacks fit this description, as many were taught to believe. When a white person would meet a black person, s/he would automatically *expect* to encounter those characteristics, or experience an "exception." In either case, cultural perceptions were at work in a prejudicial (pre-judging) way. And, black perceptions of whites took on a cultural flavor, as well. They expected the whites to have certain characteristics such as an aura of superiority, being racially prejudiced, filled with hypocricy, using power to maintain the status-quo rather than for the establishment of long-overdue justice; and they, too, sometimes experienced "exceptions," but they knew, in their hearts, that that's what they were: only "exceptions." And when a black person would meet a white person, s/he would automatically *expect* the worst as their culture had taught. In both cases, we have cultural perceptions leading to stereotyping, which, in turn, leads to prejudicial behavior.

On the first day of a new term several years ago,

Tim appeared in one of my classes—a curly-headed young man with a speech irregularity and a rather lop-sided smile, walking very haltingly with a crooked metal three-pronged cane. This was at a time when drug experimentation wasn't quite so common among "good" kids, and some very unfortunate examples of overdosing made a few students really stand out from the crowd. Tim had enough of these characteristics to make it a simple task for other students to "fill in the gaps." Tim felt rather isolated, except for a couple of students known to be drug and people users, who saw in him either a fellow traveler or a vulnerable buyer. After a few class periods, Tim appeared at my office door. He wanted to talk about the class's reaction to his being there. During his visit, Tim told me his story. He was an "A" student at a prestigious private college before transferring here, and he was on a football scholarship. On the last day of classes before Christmas break, he had been "horsing around" on the stairwell in the Student Center, when he lost his balance, fell over the railing and down three stories between the stair-casings, bouncing and breaking bones all the way down, and landing on his head and back of his neck. He had not been expected to live. During his recuperation, Tim was forced to revise his priorities in life, to redream his goals, and restructure his personality. And, no, he had never used drugs (except those necessary for rehabilitation). He wanted to tell the class his story, in hopes of reducing his sense of isolation. I suggested he wait until the next week when we would be discussing the subject of perception. I had an idea, if Tim were willing to assist, that not only would help Tim achieve his goal, but also teach the class a much needed lesson.

Immediately before I formally introduced the unit on perception to the class, I explained to them that we would participate in an interesting exercise which would directly involve everyone in the class. Everyone was to take out a blank sheet of paper on which they would write their impression of someone else in the class. This would be a particular someone, and no one would see what anyone else had written—unless, of course, someone wanted to share it voluntarily. I assured them all that the person I would name had already given his permission to be focused upon in this manner (a statement that considerably relieved a number of students). I then identified Tim as the person about whom they were to write their impression: of the kind of person he was, why he walks and talks the way he does, his abilities, his interests, and lastly, how the person writing the impression really feels about having to relate to Tim. Again, I reassured the class that only they would see what they had written. Most did not want to put down on paper what they were thinking (once down, it was difficult to deny!). However, after much urging, most of them did so. When they had finished, I asked them to put away what they had written, to look at later. Then Tim came forward and told his story. He had no more finished than the atmosphere in the room changed dramatically. They were interested in Tim as they had not been before he spoke. It was difficult to repress the questionning until I finished the exercise. I then asked the class to take out another blank sheet of paper, and write down their perception of Tim now. They did, after which I asked them to reread what they had written on the first sheet of paper, and to compare the two. If anyone was willing to share their own reaction to this exercise, and what they might have learned from it, they were invited to do so. A number of students accepted the invitation, and publicly apologized for their own behavior. It was one of the highlights of my teaching career, truly an experiment in reconciliation.

Yes, perception is a powerful force in creating and maintaining relationships. It is an aspect of communication of which a pastor needs to be very much aware. Perception creates the reality in which people live. Simon Peter perceived Jesus to be the Messiah, and thereby created the reality in which he would live. Meaning *is* perception!

However, relationships are not the only experiences in life that feel the power of perception. Our perception can both limit and expand our opportunities, mental and emotional development, and creative abilities. Sometimes we become so convinced of "can't," that we really "can't." Or at least "can't" see any way of doing it. Until we're shown that it *can* be done. I'm thinking of the simple (not simplistic!) behavior of forgiveness, so essential to the Christian Gospel. Some people do not forgive others because they cannot perceive its possibility. They might believe that Jesus forgave "because he was divine;" but it's not possible for mere human beings to forgive some people and some things. Until a person weaves the possibility into her/his worldview-tapestry, the possibility of forgiving someone simply does not exist. It seems to me that the pastor needs not only to talk about forgiveness, but also to exhibit it in life, to model it for the congregation. (A frightening thought: this could be one explanation why some pastors feel victimized by their people, that the members are really testing the pastor to see how possible forgiveness really is!)

The "nine dot puzzle" is a graphic representation of this delimiting power of perception. With four straight lines, and without lifting your pencil from the diagram, connect the following nine dots.

Most people see these nine dots as a square, as a "container" with nine spots in it. Try as they may, they cannot connect the dots by following the two simple rules stated above; that is, until they are given "permission" to draw lines "outside" the perceived container. When they understand that they are allowed to move outside the square (and that there was never a restriction against it), they alter their perception of the puzzle—and solve it.

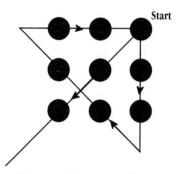

The nine dots did not change; our perception changed. Forgiveness does not change; our perception of its possibility changes. Tim didn't change; the class's perception of Tim changed. Racial and gender differences have not really changed; our perception of them have. When our perceptual reality does not jibe with factual reality or opportunity, we are limiting ourselves from reaching our full potential. This is true of us as pastors, and it is true of the people we serve. The more we incorporate this understanding into our relational behavior, the more effectively we will minister to our people.

Chapter Four
"Tell It Like It Is"

"Then the disciples came and asked him, 'Why do you speak to them in parables?'"

Matthew 13:10 NRSV

We who have been taught educational methodology claim to know the answer to the disciples' question. Among other reasons for teaching in parables: they pique curiosity; they frequently are created out of common experiences, hence are easier to remember than straight prose; and they provide opportunity for multiple application. We believe Jesus frequently taught in parables as an attempt to clarify what he was saying, as an effective teaching method. However, his answer to the disciples' question included none of the above reasons. Rather, it was even more confusing. "To you it has been given to know the secrets of the kingdom of heaven, but to them it has not been given. . .The reason I speak to them in parables is that 'seeing they do not perceive, and hearing they do not listen, nor do they understand . . .But blessed are your eyes, for they see, and your ears, for they hear." (Matthew 13:11,13,16. NRSV)

Mark, from whom Biblical scholars believe Matthew took this text, seemingly theorized differently from modern educators, concluding that Jesus' parables were really esoteric teachings, meant to be understood only by his closest disciples and not by the uninitiated. Instead of illustrating and clarifying a truth, Jesus' parables seemed to confuse many of his hearers, such confusion being one of many reasons which led to Jesus' death; that is, the people, particularly those who held the power of life and death, did not understand who he was and what he was saying to them.

Whatever Mark actually may have believed is beyond the purpose of this chapter. I chose this verse to introduce the subject of language, knowing the possibility of being accused of lifting it out of context, because Jesus' choice of words and how he used them was a stated concern of Jesus' original followers and remains a concern with us today. I might even broaden the question they raised by paraphrasing it—hopefully not losing its intended meaning: "Why do you use language as you do?"

Without answering for Jesus, let me state the obvious: all language (which includes parables) is mystifying. The choice of sounds to make words and the way we put these words together to express meaning is not an easily understood process. In fact, the use of language is a significant contributor to misunderstanding as the normal result of the communicating process, a point we made in Chapter One.

Language is symbolic, and all the problems of symbol use are included when we employ language. The general semanticists liken our use of language to our use of maps. Before we take a trip, and during it, we open a map to see what routes we will follow. The map is *not* the territory. When we move our fingers along the map tracing the route, we are not actually taking the trip; we are employing a symbolic representation of the real thing. As the map is the symbol of the territory, so our words are the symbols of the objects about which we are speaking: names, labels, general concepts, our perceptions, thoughts, feelings, moods, desires, etc. The word "points to" the object of focus; it is *not* the object of focus.

However, to say words are "only symbols" is meant in no way to suggest any lessening of language's power to influence people's behavior. We human beings live and die by symbols, especially by words as symbols. Just a few years ago, the entire world felt the tension caused by the Muslim reaction to some words in a novel written by Salomon Rushdie. Periodically, some expression about the American flag or national anthem will stir emotions to such a degree that it instigates a national debate. Epithets about one's mother have been known to start street brawls. All words; all symbols; but what power!

As users of language, pastors need to understand as much as possible about this vehicle of the Word we speak, and of the power inherent in it. In this chapter, I will attempt to highlight only a few of the many aspects of language and language-use, hopefully those which will be of most use in the pastor's communicating life in the parish. If more detail and analysis is desired, I recommend the reader seek the works of linguistic scholars and general semanticists, beginning with Mario Pei, Alfred Korzybski, and S.I. Hayakawa.

Every term I told my students in the introductory speech communication course that if they remembered nothing else, at least commit this to memory: "Words have no meaning; people do." Most of us learn just the opposite in elementary school. When little Bobby goes up to the teacher's desk at free reading time with a puzzled look on his face, and asks teacher what a certain word means, the teacher invariably says, "Go look it up in the dictionary." And Bobby does, often finding more than one "meaning" for that word in this so-called book of meanings. What Bobby does not know and what teacher does not tell him is that the dictionary is not really a book of meanings, but rather a book of common usage. Dictionary compilers provide readers with how people use words, with which "meanings" are used most often, and which next, etc. Teacher would be much more helpful—and more accurate—by sending Bobby to the dictionary, not for meaning, but to see how people often use that word; then he could discern what the author might have meant when the author used that word. By implying otherwise, teachers become unintentional perpetrators of a falsehood that causes an infinite number of communication problems.

In <u>Through the Looking Glass</u>, Lewis Carroll writes of a conversation between Alice and Humpty Dumpty:

> "I don't know what you mean by 'glory,'" Alice said. Humpty Dumpty smiled contemptuously. "Of course you don't—till I tell you. I meant 'there's a nice knock-down argument for you!'"
>
> "But 'glory' doesn't mean 'a nice knock-down argument,'" Alice objected.
>
> "When I use a word," Humpty Dumpty said, in a rather scornful tone, "it means just what I choose it to mean—neither more nor less."
>
> "The question is," said Alice, "whether you <u>can</u> make words mean so many different things."
>
> "The question is," said Humpty Dumpty, "which is to be master—that's all."

Meanings of words are in the intent of the user, whether it be Humpty Dumpty, Alice, Lewis Carroll, the pastor of the church, or any layperson within that church.

A phrase well known to all, and whose meaning is "crystal clear," illustrates this point. We all know what "I love you" means. James Meerloo, in

Conversation and Communication, writes

> ..."I love you" is a statement that can be expressed in
> so many varied ways. It may be a stage song, repeated
> daily without any meaning, or a barely audible murmur,
> full of surrender. Sometimes it means: "I desire you" or
> "I want you sexually." It may mean: "I hope you love
> me" or "I hope that I will be able to love you." Often it
> means: "It may be that a love relationship can develop
> between us" or even "I hate you." Often it is a wish for
> emotional exchange: "I want your admiration in
> exchange for mine" or "I give my love in exchange for
> some passion" or "I want to feel cozy and at home with
> you" or "I admire some of your qualities." A declaration
> of love is mostly a request: "I desire you" or "I want you
> to gratify me," or "I want your protection" or "I want to
> be intimate with you" or "I want to exploit your
> loveliness."
>   Sometimes it is the need for security and tenderness,
> for parental treatment. It may mean: "My self-love goes
> out to you." But it may also express submissiveness:
> "Please take me as I am," or "I feel guilty about you; I
> want, through you, to correct the mistakes I have made
> in human relations." It may be self-sacrifice and a
> masochistic wish for dependency. However, it may also
> be a full affirmation of the other, taking the
> responsibility for mutual exchange of feelings. It may
> be a weak feeling of friendliness, it may be the scarcely
> even whispered expression of ecstasy. "I love you,"—
> wish, desire, submission, conquest; it is never the word
> itself that tells the real meaning here.

Just how crystal clear is this very common
expression? I have an unproven theory—a hunch—
that we humans use this particular expression in
many instances simply *because* its meaning is so
varied and unclear. Once said, we can always deny
we meant how the other person understood it; that
is, if the developing relationship isn't working out

as we had imagined or hoped. (Examples abound in marital and divorce counseling!) "I love you" is sometimes used as a "trial balloon" to define a relationship. Of course, this is only a "hunch" on my part. However, other expressions can also be included under the category of "deniable meanings," from the ritualistic "Stop by anytime" (do so at 3AM and see if "anytime" is really what the person meant!) to "No more taxes" (does this include "user-fees?"). "Of course, pastor, I believe in attending church *regularly*" (meaning every Christmas and Easter, unless something comes up). I have heard a number of pastors express frustration over the many evening and weekend meetings they must attend as part of their pastoral responsibilities and bemoan the little amount of time they do spend with their families. "I don't have much time to be with my children; I do, rather, believe in *quality* time" (does "believing" include "doing?" and who and what determines "quality?").

"Deniable meanings" is only part of the broader subject of "metatalk," jargon for "more than one level of meaning," depending on context and/or manner of delivery. Judith Martin in <u>Miss Manners' Guide to Excruciatingly Correct Behavior</u> offers numerous examples of this metatalk.

> "Call me." This can mean "Don't bother me now—let's discuss it on office time," or "I would accept if you asked me out" or "I can't discuss this here" or "Don't go so fast."

"I'll call you." This has opposite meanings, and you have to judge by the delivery. One is "Let's start something" and the other is "Don't call me."

"Please come and stay with me." Said to someone from another area, this means "I would consider extending an invitation at your convenience if it coincides with my convenience."

"Let's have lunch." Among social acquaintances, this means "If you ever have nothing to do on a day I have nothing to do, let's get together." Among business acquaintances, it means "If you have something useful to say to me I'll listen."

"We really must see more of each other." One of the tricky ones, this actually means "I can't make the time to see you."

"We must do this more often." Another variation. This one is really "This was surprisingly enjoyable, but it's still going to happen infrequently."

Sometimes meaning is wrapped up in a whole body of words. I recall visiting a newcomer to our parish. She and her family had attended worship service on the previous Sunday. She was not happy with the experience. Oh, the people were friendly, all right; the music was inspiring; even the sermon was helpful. She was, however, very disappointed that we did not say the Apostles' Creed in the liturgy, but used one of the other creeds from our hymnal (that Sunday being the Nicene Creed). I explained that we alternated the historic creeds from season to season, and that the ones we used all expressed approximately the same beliefs, the basic criteria being the historic affirmation of the Faith. This explanation was unacceptable to her. Only the Apostles' Creed had "religious" meaning for her. The same words, organized differently, even those which might have more historical validity, simply were "wrong." I referred her to another church in town where the Apostles' Creed was spoken on a regular basis. The level of meaning at which this woman was operating was quite different from mine, and on a subject that was obviously so very important to her worship-life.

We cannot leave the topic of "meaning" before we look at its two basic parts: denotation and connotation. Simply stated, denotation is the most commonly accepted dictionary definition of a word (most often the first one given when there is a list of usage possibilities). "Cross," according to Webster, is "a gibbet or ancient instrument of torture, generally made of two pieces of timber placed across each other, usually with an upright set in the ground and a horizontal crosspiece below the top of the upright; upon this, criminals were in ancient times nailed or bound and left to die." This is a fair denotative meaning of the word "cross." However, to most Christians, that is not the whole meaning of the word, nor even the most important part of the meaning. There's much more to it than that; the connotative meaning must be added. Most Christians will look at a cross and see "the place where Jesus died" and, more connotatively, "where

Jesus died for *my* sins." Connotation is the "emotional overlay" people give to the word/symbols they use, and by far carries most of the word's weight in power and influence.

When we choose the words to convey our ideas, especially we who live in the public eye, we need to be aware of the connotative power of our words and that it is this connotation that carries the greatest impact in our conversations and speaking, regardless of how the dictionary defines the words. And we can never be absolutely certain what anyone's emotional overlay on any particular word is, because it depends on that person's experience with that word, or with the concept or object which is symbolized by that word. However, we can and do guess at the emotion such a word generates, using our experience with probabilities, formed by our own observations and studies of human behavior. We must realize, though, that our guesses are just that: guesses.

We know there are certain words that evoke strong emotional responses. We call these "red flag words." The wise pastor will be aware of this. Periodically for more than three decades, one of my former teaching colleagues took an informal survey of his students on the connotative power of certain words. I, too, did the same thing, although less systematically than he. Our results, however, were very similar. Years ago, in the 1950's, the word which generated the most negative emotion was "communist." That changed over the years. In the late 1980's, the word which generated the most negative emotion was "gay." The years in between saw "hippie," "nigger," "pig," "feminist," "redneck," "peace," each take its turn. The denotative meaning of these words remained the same; however, the connotative meaning changed. The emotional overlay, the first line of reaction, alters as human beings experience their world. Experiencing a new event and/or an altered relationship can change a person's meaning of the word which was once used to describe such an event or relationship. The word, with the new experience added to it, stimulates the emotions generated from that experience, which in turn generate the reaction. In the 1988 presidential campaign, the word "liberal" was used effectively as a symbol which pulled negative emotions from many citizens. In using the word, George Bush was communicating primarily on the connotative level. Michael Dukakis, in countering the power of this word, tried to respond first on the denotative level, but was unsuccessful until he switched to emphasizing the positive emotion also in the word and tradition, the connotative level, the first line of reaction.

Even with the ecumenical spirit that seems to be alive in many of our churches today, there are still numerous examples of resistance to that spirit. The Apostles' Creed provides one of them. In some

Protestant traditions, there are a few people who still refuse to say "the holy catholic church," and change it to "the holy Christian church," solely because of their long-standing emotional resistance to anything "Catholic." Even when such people are taught the denotative difference between "catholic" and "Catholic," their emotional overlay is so strong that they will not change their behavior. In my first year of teaching I had a young freshman student who "needed to talk" about a communication problem she was having. She was "at odds" with her family over religion. Brought up a Roman Catholic, attending parochial schools all her life thus far, she was having difficulty handling the pluralism of the state university. She did not know, nor did I tell anyone in that class my first year of teaching, that I was also a Protestant clergyman. During our periodic conversations over the next few weeks, she seemed more able to work out her problems with her parents, and was more comfortable relating to them and to her church than she was at the beginning of the term when she first came to me seeking help. On the final day of class, I shared with the students that I was an ordained United Methodist minister, and hoped that my personal religious faith had not been a barrier to their learning over the term, and maybe had even enhanced it a bit. Most of the class was surprised, and a number of students assured me there was no barrier. I noticed that my young friend was very quiet and did not respond, even though she had become quite verbal over the term. After class I stopped her to chat for a moment, and, my curiosity getting the best of me, I commented on her lack of verbal reaction to my self-disclosure. Her response was most interesting: "If you had told me you were a Protestant minister, it would have made no difference; however, if you would have said you were a 'Methodist,' I probably would have dropped the class!" She was not angry, only confused—she was wrestling with her emotional overlay to the word "Methodist." We did chat later from time to time, and frequently laughed about this experience, discovering the roots of her reaction in an experience as a young girl when she had a Methodist neighbor who was constantly trying to convert her. She had built an emotional overlay to the word "Methodist" that was beyond the denotative meaning of the word, and influenced her reactions to anything "Methodist."

Another place where connotative power is evident is in the use of emotive words to describe something or someone. What might sound like fact often is but an announcement of the speaker's attitude toward the person, concept, or object being described. S.I. Hayakawa has suggested that the practice of "conjugating irregular verbs" might have originated with Bertrand Russell, although I suspect it may have been around long before his time. The technique is uncomplicated; it merely involves taking an action or personality trait and viewing it in varying degrees of favorability, according to the label we give it. Adler and Towne offer some interesting examples:

> I read love stories.
> You read erotic literature.
> She reads pornography.
>
> I'm thrifty.
> You're money conscious.
> He's a tightwad.
>
> I'm casual.
> You're a little careless. (I prefer: You're extremely informal.)
> He's a slob.

We could add a few interesting ones, too. "I'm traditional. You're conservative. He's reactionary." Or, "I'm a born-again Christian. You're a member of a Christian Church. She goes to church." Or, "I'm overworked. You take on extra tasks. She finds things to fill up her time." Or, "I run a tight ship. You demand that all rules be followed. He's a dictator." With tongue in cheek, Adler and Towne (Looking Out, Looking In, 6th ed.) "help" us to see the difference between a businessman and a businesswoman:

> A businessman is aggressive; a businesswoman is pushy.
> He is careful about details; she's picky.
> He loses his temper because he's so involved in his job; she's bitchy.

He's depressed (or hung over), so everyone tiptoes past
   his office; she's moody, so it must be her time of the
   month.
He follows through; she doesn't know when to quit.
He's firm; she's stubborn.
He makes wise judgments; she reveals her prejudices.
He is a man of the world; she's been around.
He isn't afraid to say what he thinks; she's opinionated.
He exercises authority; she's tyrannical.
He's discreet; she's secretive.
He's a stern taskmaster; she's difficult to work for.

With the dramatic increase of enrollment of women in our seminaries, I suspect the above "comparison" may not be limited to the field of business. Unfortunately, some church people may well be viewing female pastors in a similar vein. We need to remember that the use of emotive words reflects the speaker's attitudes and is not an actual description, and that the connotative power of words is far greater than the denotative power, and we need to be both careful and wise in our employment of them.

"Naming" is a fascinating aspect of language use, and follows naturally on the heels of our discussion on the use of verbs and adjectives. We have already alluded to the power of naming in our discussion of words that evoke negative emotional reactions. Naming an action, a role, a person, an event will influence how those are perceived. Most of us have become acquainted with the change of names from "trash collector" to "sanitation engineer." And we sometimes chuckle at the "ridiculousness" of such a name-change; yet we know it does make a difference. A revered politician almost seems a contradiction in terms, so we call that person a "statesman." A phone solicitor is now called a "telemarketing representative;" an inspector is a "quality assurance technician;" a salesperson is a "marketing specialist." Just recently my wife was speaking with the mother of seven who referred to herself not as a housewife or even as a homemaker, but rather as a "homemaking engineer." Even the name of the local church's clergyperson makes a difference in how that person is perceived and how s/he perceives the self. Will it be "pastor?" or "reverend?" or "doctor?" or "brother/sister?" or "father/mother?" or "Mr./Mrs./Ms.?" or "Pastor Pat?" or "Dr. Bob?" or just plain "Dick or Barb?" Whatever name is preferred and used, an image and a role will certainly develop from it.

Over the last forty years a large segment of our population has been struggling with this naming phenomenon. The larger of the three groups to which I am referring here has accepted names varying from negro to Negro to colored to Black to African American. Each name reflects some aspect of their heritage or a Caucasion perception to which they needed to respond. The word-symbol name reflects an identity which communicates a message to both members and nonmembers of the race. I am reminded of an anecdote reputed to come from the life of Martin Luther King, Jr. Someone once asked him if he minded being called "colored," to which he replied, "Not when the alternative is colorless." A second racial group with a changing referrent name is Hispanic, or Chicano, or Latin American, or Spanish American. A third group is sometimes called American Indians and sometimes Native Americans. Occasionally, they are referred to by their tribal identities: e.g., Objibway (Chippewa), Iroquois, Apache, Dakota, Cherokee, Navajo, Inuit. Minority groups seem to have greater need for self-imposed name identity since it gives them some control over communicating who they are to the majority. Pastors, as well as all others concerned about human relations, need to be aware of the power of racial and cultural group names and exercise wisdom in the use of them.

Another phenomenon of language use which occasionally creates problems seems to be the distinguishing of facts from inferences, or rather the failure to do so. More of our speaking relies on inferences than we are prone to admit. Our minds, for the sake of efficiency, shortcut the movement from fact to fact, and make assumptions of connections that are not necessarily accurate. If I were to tell you about seeing Barb Jones' car in front of the church on Tuesday morning from 10 to 11 AM (the *fact?*), and share my knowledge about Barb having problems relating to her teenage son, and we both know that Pastor Sam is an excellent counselor on family relationships, we might conclude that Barb is being counseled by Pastor Sam and the subject is relating to her teenage son. However, most of that, particularly the conclusion, is inference, not fact. Barb's husband, Dick, is a plumber. The company truck is in the shop for repairs, so he is driving Barb's automobile. It's an inference that Barb is the driver. It seems that Pastor Sam, when he arrived Tuesday morning, discovered the toilets overflowing, so he called Dick. It's an inference that Barb would ask Pastor Sam to talk with her about her son. It's an inference that what we were told about their family tension is actually true. It is even an inference that the car belongs to Barb Jones; she may have sold it over the weekend.

We can tie together the naming and the inference phenomena by focusing on the word "is," one of the most troublesome words in the English language (and there are equivalent words in other languages, too). Someone once summarized the problem as "the trouble with 'is' is 'is.'" "Is" implies "equals"—this *is* that; this *equals* that. Ronnie is an American. Norm is a Baptist. Shirley is a good mother. Janelle is a fledgling attorney. Yet, it would be far more accurate to acknowledge that there "is" more in each person than the "is" indicates. Also, especially when an adjective is attached, we assume that each has all the qualities of the other: all American qualities are in Ronnie; all Baptist characteristics are in Norm; everything about a good mother is true of Shirley; all traits of "fledglingness" as well as our perception of an attorney is true of Janelle. Then we can add to the simple observable problem of equivalency the problem of time and situation. Ronnie will immigrate to Canada next month. Next year *is* Ronnie an American? Norm is a Baptist who regularly attends an Episcopal Church. What is he in that situation: a Baptist Episcopalian? Shirley wants to spend less time with her children and more time on her career. Does a diminished nurturing desire negate the "isness" of Shirley's good motherliness? Of course, this discussion is silly. If we know what we mean, why all this concern about a two-letter word? Only because of its often negative effect on people.

When we hear the word "is" connected to roles, behaviors, and characteristics, we need to recognize that such communication behavior tends to delimit a person, "pigeonhole" human beings, and impose definitions on people. It *sounds* like a fact, often like an absolute! Paul *is* lazy (when? under what circumstances? based on what criteria? with what definition? in whose judgment?). Sharon *is* an effective leader (in every situation? all the time? in whose judgment? according to what criteria?). John *is* a funny man (never serious? in whose judgment? definition of "funny?"). I'm not suggesting we get rid of the verb "to be," only that we recognize its effect on the truth of our statements and on the negative impact it may have on others.

Using overly abstract words seems to be a common behavior of many people in the clergy. Maybe it's our way of not being "pinned down." We seem to use the words "peace," "love," "sacrifice," "brotherhood," and "service," more than we talk about a specific nuclear test ban agreement, a particular behavior which expresses affection, giving up a specific something of great personal value in order to achieve something significant for someone else, meeting occasionally with a family of another religion or race in order to know and understand each other, or taking a turn at delivering "meals on wheels" to the homebound. The former is abstract religion; the latter is concrete religion. The former tends to stagnate in words; the latter tends to vibrate with life. The former is relatively safe to discuss; the latter changes lives and "turns the world upside down." The more concrete and less abstract our words, the more powerful our witness.

A subject on which we could spend pages is our use of euphemisms both in our private conversations and in our public speaking. By euphemism I mean a word or phrase which is substituted for another word or phrase with which the speaker is uncomfortable in a particular setting. I illustrate with a concept with which our society is most uncomfortable, a concept with which the pastor works frequently: death. Depending upon the situation, the people involved in the conversation, and the background of the speaker, we will hear death referred to as: "sleeping;" "gone to their reward;" "kicked the bucket;" "bought the farm;" "with Jesus;" "gone;" "at peace;" "six feet under;" "departed;" "pushing up daisies;" etc. When the pastor hears such euphemisms used regularly, it is an indication of the difficulty in handling the subject of death, an awareness which might lead to some parish education on the concept. There are other general subject categories that sometimes cause discomfort when discussed. Our society is very uncomfortable talking about the human body, particularly the genital area and the process of waste elimination. We teach our children such labels as "wee-wee," "peter," "down there," later to be changed to "cock," "dong," "cunt," but how seldom do we hear "penis" and "vagina?" Why do we shy away from using the biological and generally understood denotative names? The answer we have been given, and it makes sense, is that we are uncomfortable with the subject, and the euphemism is a way of decreasing the discomfort. Other categories in which we frequently find euphemisms are in the abuse of alcohol, sexual behavior, spouse labels, and war.

Thus far we have seen how human beings, through euphemisms, abstractions, naming, deliberate metatalk, irregular verb conjugation, and numerous other linguistic devices often use language to protect themselves from the reality they fear, rather than as a vehicle of reconciliation and a way to reduce the feeling of isolation we all have. Aldous Huxley, in writing about the language of war in <u>Words and Behavior</u>, concludes with the following:

> We protect our minds by an elaborate system of abstractions, ambiguities, metaphors and similes from the reality we do not wish to know too clearly; we lie to ourselves, in order that we may still have the excuse of ignorance, the alibi of stupidity and incomprehension, (so that) we can continue with a good conscience to commit and tolerate the most monstrous crimes.

As Huxley so ably implies, whole cultures make extensive use of language's protective qualities. In Chapter Two we discussed the Whorfian hypothesis, looking at the influence of language on self-concept (the "Experience in Awareness" article). Tying grammatical correctness into the use of the masculine pronoun in place of developing or borrowing from another language an all-inclusive pronoun for both males and females has been one way of our culture's protecting the status quo view of sexual roles, power, and importance. When a culture teaches its young by identifying the highlights of history according to the wars it has fought, by its choice of word-symbols, it is protecting its cultural self-image as a justly violent people. It seems to me that part of the prophetic responsibility of the parish minister is to alert the people to what is being reinforced through their use of language, and to challenge them to evaluate their collective behavior. Pastors, as they speak interpersonally and publicly, also need to be aware themselves of their own possible reinforcing word choices. Are the words and expressions we choose to convey our ideas inadvertantly reinforcing cultural concepts that are really contrary to some of our most cherished values?

When pastors speak, particularly in public, they open themselves to criticism from their congregation. A major part of the impression we make on others is based on how we speak, that is, on our use of language. Since language is "rule governed" (grammar), people "worth listening to" partially indicate this worthiness by their knowledge of and adherence to the rules. Someone who "don't speak good" won't receive the same positive attention as someone who does speak well. It is a wise pastor who knows the rules and breaks them only occasionally.

Dialect also affects impressions and listenability. Regional dialect will reflect to a listener the cultural characteristics perceived to be held by the people of that region. One of my sons transferred to a college in Texas. Being a native of Minnesota, he spoke like a northerner from the midwest. As a theatre major, he auditioned for numerous parts, always to be assigned the role of the villain or the antagonist, but never the protagonist lead, roles that he was frequently assigned in the northern college he attended. In frustration he confronted the directing professor, asking why this was so. He was told to seek the services of a speech therapist if he wanted to be a hero on stage, because the way he talked (his dialect) was not the way any Texas hero would talk, and he simply wouldn't be believable to a Texas audience. Perceived cultural characteristics are carried by one's dialect, whether it be on stage or in the pulpit. A pastor should be prepared for this kind of reaction by some members of a congregation, especially if the pastor were to move from one geographical region to another.

Another kind of dialect that affects how others see a pastor might be labeled a "preaching dialect." With some clergy such a manner of delivery is as observable outside the pulpit as it is in it. Whenever and wherever these preachers have an audience, their voice pitch rises, volume increases, the words chosen are more complex, an attitude of pontificating is perceived. Their dialect betrays their vocation.

The final point I would make on language usage is how it reflects relationships. The ideas we share, the words we choose, and how we speak those words—all are indicators of the relationship the speaker has with the audience, be it an audience of one or one thousand. Our language, in a very real sense, structures our relationships, from the ritualistic "How are you today?" to the quietly spoken concern "I noticed a tear in your eye when

I told that story; would you like to talk about it?" The more ritualistic our speaking, the more distance between communicators; the less ritualistic, the less interpersonal distance.

What we consider appropriate language will vary with our perceived relationship. I've heard a few pastors bemoan the fact that no one in their congregation will tell an off-color joke in their presence. Their unwillingness to do so indicates something about their relationship with the pastor. With some people in the parish a pastor will speak only about theology and church business; with others, anything and everything, from politics to sports; again, relationships being defined by language appropriateness. When two or more clergypersons are together, their language will often reflect their relationship in their use of jargon. Words pulled from their vocational specialization will indicate to each other and to anyone outside the conversation what their relationship is, and probably communicate to that outside person how welcome s/he is to become part of that relationship.

Lastly, the degree of formality in language usage will reflect the relationship, particularly the role structure. We raised our children at a time when we believed they should call all adults "Mr. or Mrs." or some other title of respect. When our oldest son went to college, his advisor wanted to be called by her first name, a request that caused him great discomfort. A first name basis with one's adult teacher was not what he had learned as a child at home. She didn't have her PhD, else he could have called her "Dr." She was married, but kept her original last name; so "Mrs." was not appropriate. She disliked "Ms." and would not answer to it. He was in a dilemma. How could he express his formal relationship in a title when his advisor preferred a less formal relationship and the language to go along with it?

Style of speaking is another indicator of the degree of formality and thus of relationship. When a person speaks in longer, more complex and grammatically precise sentences, that person is establishing a more formal and more distant relationship with the audience. When the sentences are simpler, seemingly more spontaneous, and idiomatic, a less formal relationship is believed to exist. Pastors, by their use of language, can, in large part, define the kind of relationship they want both with individuals in their parish and with their assembled congregations on public speaking occasions.

Language certainly is mystifying, and our use of it is not an easily understood process. The foregoing discussion underscores why this aspect of communication is such a significant contributor to misunderstanding, and why this most common tool of the pastor is so fraught with both problems and possibilities.

Chapter Five
"Actions Speak Louder Than Words"

"When he was at table with them, he took bread, blessed
and broke it, and gave it to them. Then their eyes were
opened, and they recognized him. . .Then they told what
had happened on the road, and how he had been made
known to them in the breaking of the bread."
Luke 24:30,31,35 NRSV

These two men whom Jesus joined on the walk
to Emmaus did not hear Jesus' words, their
depression over recent events preventing this, but
they did recognize Jesus' actions. Words could not
penetrate their emotional condition; nonverbal
behavior could and did. They did not understand
Jesus' explanation, his putting events in
perspective, even as clear as it might be to us who
read this account almost two thousand years later.
However, when Jesus demonstrated who he was
by *doing* something with which they had experience
and could identify, these two men began to
understand. This is one example of actions
speaking louder than words: the power of nonverbal
communication.

What exactly constitutes "nonverbal

communication?" One of the better definitions I've found is "messages expressed by nonlinguistic means" to which I would add "that are interpreted by a receiver on the basis of the receiver's own experience." Paraphrased, we're talking about communication by means other than words or spoken language (with one exception, paralanguage, which will be discussed later in this chapter).

Why should an awareness of nonverbal communication be important to a pastor? For a number of reasons. One: to raise to conscious level the inadvertent messages one is sending to others, and if necessary, to adjust them. Two: to gain insight into the more subtly expressed needs of others in order to minister more effectively. Three: to prevent the pastor from being overly influenced by the topic's often less-than-well-researched coverage in the popular press.

Albert Mehrabian, a psychologist who has studied nonverbal communication extensively, claims that 93% of the emotional impact of a message is transmitted by nonverbal means! Other researchers in the field suggest that it's less, but no one suggests less than 65%. In any case, it is no wonder we have developed the folk-saying, "Actions speak louder than words." Words and language (spoken and written) convey thoughts and ideas; nonverbals transmit feelings. Possibly, if we only related to machines, this division would be inconsequential. It wouldn't matter what the nonverbal did or did not do. However, we relate to human beings who have feelings, and whose feelings are often more important to them, to us, and to our relationship than ideas and concepts are. Hence, any pastor should be intensely aware of that 65% to 93% of the message.

Nonverbals are not suited to conveying thoughts and ideas; that seems to be why language was developed. Try describing Tillich's <u>Shaking of the Foundations</u> without using words! Or Niebuhr's <u>Christ and Culture</u>; or Fletcher's <u>Situation Ethics</u>! It would be ludicrous and a waste of time even to try. Nonverbal messages are primarily attitudinal; they do not convey the idea, but rather an attitude toward the idea, or toward the self, or toward the hearers, or toward the relationship, or toward the situation. By the eyes, the posture, the clothing, the edge in the voice, the breathing pattern, and a host of other wordless vehicles, the communicator's attitude (and broader message) is conveyed.

Nonverbals are "culture-bound;" that is to say, they are developed within a specific culture, and do not necessarily have the same meaning in another culture. Use of certain gestures by international tourists have created numerous funny and some not-so-funny situations. International and intercultural businesspeople have discovered that not every human being sees time or distance the same way. The meaning and intensity of eye contact varies around the world. Some behaviors, though having similar meaning to most people everywhere, simply are not situationally appropriate to some while they are to others—because the culture in which they were raised taught them so. Different cultures have developed different "rules" for appropriate behavior, verbal and nonverbal, and breaking these rules will have consequences, as Edward T. Hall observed in <u>The Silent Language</u>, and <u>The Hidden Dimension</u>, and others have observed since Hall's seminal work. With the world fast becoming more and more a "global village," and increasing numbers of our people being interculturally mobile, it is wise for the pastor to be aware of how culturally bound nonverbal communication really is.

Nonverbal communication is ambiguous. Anyone who is attempting to become more aware of this facet of communication needs to develop a "checking-out" skill. We should look at nonverbals as "clues" to be verified. For example, the crossing of the arms in front of one's chest may mean "I don't agree with you," or it may mean "I'm chilly" (temperature-wise), or "I'm nervous, and I don't know what to do with my hands," or any of a number of things. Before adjusting the verbal message, the effective communicator will try to discover what the other person means by the crossed arms. Not only is ambiguity communicated when a nonverbal behavior could be interpreted in more than one way, but also when the nonverbal message contradicts the verbal message, as sometimes occurs. When the words indicate one thing, but the person does not look you in the eye, most people in our culture receive contradictory messages: truthful words and lying eyes. The normal (natural?) tendency seems to be to believe the eyes and not the words, as in another folk-saying: "Your actions speak so loudly, I can't hear a word you're saying." The less-than-effective communicator will continue to concentrate on the ambiguous nonverbals, interpreting them according to her/his own past culturally-based experience, rather than checking out the observed disparity of messages. The lowered eyes could be a sign of respect, as it is in some cultures, or fear, if a power-relationship is present. The interpreted "lying eyes" could have nothing at all to do with the truth of the words. Failure to check-out nonverbal messages can damage relationships and adversely affect opportunities to minister.

Pastors, and all professional communicators, should be wary of the numerous popular-press books on nonverbal communication in the bookstores. They are not all equal. Some of them are downright dangerous. Few of these mass-market writings are solidly based on communication research beyond some half-truths highlighted to titillate the reader. Most seem concerned more with sales than with helping people in their relationships, catering more to the human desire to control other people than to helping them communicate more effectively.

There are three basic categories of nonverbal communication: kinesics, proxemics, and paralanguage. Other miscellaneous categories (e.g., color, use of time, body adornment, physical attractiveness) will be discussed later.

Kinesics are primarily those nonverbals related to bodily stance and movement. Gestures, both purposeful and not, are a significant part of the kinesics category. These are often accompaniments to the verbal message, but can also substitute for a verbal message. The shrug of the shoulders with the palms of the hands extended is often used to reinforce an "I don't know" response, or it can be used in place of words to express relatively the same message. Without words it could even mean "I don't care," a different message entirely. Gestures are the most obvious culture-bound category in kinesics. A number of years ago when I, a product of Northern New York State, was getting acquainted with a man who grew up in Montana, I had an experience which illustrates this very well. Chuck and I were new colleagues at the university and just beginning what has developed into a lifelong friendship. On this Friday afternoon I stopped by his office just to relax a moment and pass the time of day, and he asked me what I had planned for the weekend, to which I responded with a nonverbal gesture: I raised my hand, arm bent at the elbow, first and little finger raised straight, with thumb holding down the two middle fingers, and at the wrist moved the hand back and forth from side to side. Chuck looked at me with a most quizzical expression, and asked me, with a bit of an edge on his voice, what I meant by that. I thought everyone knew what that gesture meant: I was "on the horns of a dilemma," in this case, making up my mind between two very distinct activities. He laughed and asked me if I knew what that same gesture meant in his home region in Montana. I didn't; so he told me. It was equivalent to the middle finger extended by itself. I had given him "the finger!" What a way to begin a friendship! As we laughed about that, our imaginations began to hold sway. Imagine a group of people from his region of Montana for the first time watching a football game between the Universities of Oklahoma and Texas on television. The camera pans the Texas fans during a moment of high emotion when they are involved in a common cheer. They see thousands of people gesturing with the sign of the Texas Longhorns, the same sign I used to convey "on the horns of a dilemma," and which Chuck translated as "the finger." It's not difficult to imagine what kind of image those Montanans would be building of those vulgar Texans. Had Chuck not checked-out the meaning of my gesture, we might not be enjoying a friendship today!

I have in my personal library a paperback titled The International Dictionary of Sign Language, a book which illustrates and describes hundreds of gestures common to cultures around the world. It is amazing how many gestures there are, and how many different meanings they convey. Included are gestures of the hands, arms and fingers, the angle and movement of the head, the positioning of the body, and combinations of each. One fact I found particularly interesting is the high number of vulgar expressions transmitted by gestures, a point, I believe, important for any public communicator to know, especially one who travels from one culture to another. Enough distractions already exist to the messages a pastor shares without adding the distraction of inadvertant vulgar gestures!

One's posture and physical bearing can give off interpreted messages. In a counseling situation, the counselor who slouches in the chair says something different to the counselee than someone who sits upright and leans forward a bit. The pastor with a shuffling gait conveys a different message than does someone walking with a brisk step. The person who converses shoulder to shoulder or at an angle conveys a different message than someone who converses "straight on" in a face-to-face position.

We in the dominant North American culture put great emphasis on the face and eyes as vehicles of nonverbal messages. We have been taught that positive eye contact transmits a message of truth, integrity, and interest. However, we have all met people who can look a person right in the eye and tell a bold-faced lie. The preacher frequently addresses a congregation of interested faces and wandering minds. We have learned our lesson well: it is appropriate behavior in church to feign interest even when bored; meaning don't fidget, look in the general direction of the pulpit, and periodically nod our heads in acknowledgment (timed if possible with a general audible response of others in the congregation to something the preacher has said)— not unlike feigned listening in the classroom. Sometimes "the shoe is on the other foot" when the minister is making a pastoral visit and hears a familiar story, only with a different cast of characters. The mind wanders, but the face and eyes look interested and even give encouragement to the storyteller. The pastoral counselor, through eye contact, can influence how much a parishoner self-discloses: the higher amount and intensity of direct gaze tends to stimulate a higher degree of self-disclosure. The counselor whose eye wanders out the window or to the clock on the wall will not draw much self-disclosure from the person in the chair opposite.

Then there's communication by way of touch, another category of kinesics. Many researchers and theorists have concluded that we are a tactile-starved culture, that most of the communication by touch many of us experience is when it is accompanied by extreme passion; it's either sexually motivated or violent (sometimes both). The reassuring touch or the comforting arm across the shoulders is frequently lost and in its place we substitute a word or two. A comforting Hallmark card in the mailbox is substituted for a hug. Our Puritan forebears are usually blamed for this historical trend away from physical touching; be that accurate or not, whoever did start it did us a great disservice. Ashley Montagu's seminal work on <u>Touching</u> is something every pastor should read and read again. (For the pastor who doesn't want that long a disciplined reading, a short educational film by the same title has been made of his work and I recommend it highly.) Since study after study has determined our human need for touching behavior, it is unfortunate that a parallel concern has developed in our American society, a development that coincides with the association of touching with sexual behavior: our justifiable fear of being accused of sexual harassment or abuse, to the extent that many companies that insure churches normally now include (or exclude) sexual harassment accusation protection in their policies.

Certainly, pastors need to be concerned about their touching communication; however, they should also realize how much their people need to be touched. That line between touching-use and touching-abuse is a line that must be negotiated by every pastor who, in the fulfilling of parish responsibilities, wants to communicate personal concern and caring to the members of a congregation. There is nothing, in my opinion, that can substitute for a good hug in communicating a caring relationship; yet, in giving the hug, I realize the pastor becomes very vulnerable to misinterpretation. A hug, as any kind of touching behavior, needs not only to be given warmly and sincerely, but also wisely.

One place where physical presence, a touch, and frequently a hug is most appropriate and gratefully received is at a funeral. Very few worded expressions of sympathy are ever remembered, but a person's presence is. Many people will avoid attending a wake or coming to the funeral parlors because they "don't know what to say." However, the family of the deceased seldom remembers anyone's words, but they will recall and appreciate someone's physical presence, and a sympathetic embrace that communicates far more than a few words would ever communicate. Cradling a dying boy in my arms communicated far more to him and to his parents than any words I could have uttered, no matter how profound they might have been. Standing by a bedside saying a prayer without touching the patient seems incongrous to me. I'm convinced there is healing in the human touch, a healing not found in words alone. I believe

103

we pastors need to remember the power of touch.

I've attended worship services in churches where touching was an integral part of the people's greeting-behavior, both during the liturgy and after the service, and I've attended worship services in churches where all the greeting was verbal. The touching, most often in the form of a handshake but occasionally an embrace, made a difference in my response to that church and congregation. Touching communicated a caring attitude. The touching church seemed the warmer church attended by caring people.

The second basic category of nonverbal communication is called "proxemics," how the use of space transmits attitudinal and relational messages. I think this is the most overlooked category in nonverbal communication. The classic labeling of communiation distance is "intimate" (0-2 feet), "personal" (2-4 feet), "social" (4-12 feet), and "public" (12-25 feet, or with a public address system 12-??? feet). The physical distance between people determines the degree of intimacy in a communication relationship. Here again, one's inculturation will greatly influence which distances will be used by interactors in particular situations. The person with a Latin American upbringing will feel much more comfortable being physically closer to another human being than will someone raised in a northern European culture. Whereas the Latin converses more often at the outer limits of the "intimate" distance, the European (especially the Anglo/Germanic/Scandinavian) is much more comfortable at the outer limits of the "personal" distance, or even at the "social" distance. Edward T. Hall in his <u>Silent Language</u> generalizes his observations of North American and South American businessmen conversing. After only a few minutes, participants often find themselves at a considerable distance from where they started talking, having done what might be called a "cultural communication dance." As the South American steps toward the other in an attempt to become more comfortable with less distance between them, the North American steps backwards in an attempt to become more comfortable with more distance between them. To the South American, the other person is "cold" and "aloof." To the North American, the other is "pushy" and "aggressive." The distance between them delivers a message.

A young elementary school principal attended a summer-session class I taught on "Communicating in the Classroom." Proxemics was a major unit in that course, and one interesting discussion centered around what the placement of a desk communicated to anyone entering the office. That fall, when the new school year began, this principal moved his desk from the center of the room to a place against the wall, allowing the teacher or student who entered to sit in a chair opposite the principal with no desk in between them as a barrier. Today, after many years and a few office moves, the basic arrangement of his workspace remains as he changed it. Why? Because the desk actually did serve as a barrier between him and others, a barrier that did not exist when the people sat in chairs with only open space between them. Teachers and students felt more welcome in his office with the new arrangement of furniture; they felt that he cared more for them and what they had to say.

As a young pastor doing counseling I was not above experimenting to find more effective approaches to the counseling task. One "experiment" I conducted involved the placement of my study furniture. Like that young principal, I discovered that removing a large desk from between the counselee and myself created a more intimate and caring atmosphere. I moved the furniture in stages—over many months with different counselees, both singly and as couples: the counselee's chair from the other side of the desk, to beside the desk, to face to face with me, then both of us away from the desk altogether, then across a low coffee table, then chair to chair with only open space between us. Each stage seemed to communicate a different degree of caring. The use of space in my study communicated a message.

I had a fascinating experience with proxemics as a pastor in a building program. The plans for the costly sanctuary/office project were progressing surprisingly well, until the designing of the chancel area. The Building Committee was divided sharply on the placement of the pastor's chair/pew, where the pastor would sit when not directly leading the liturgy. Half of the committee wanted the seat elevated above the congregation "because the pastor should be considered above the members of the congregation, both in importance and in moral behavior." The other half (with whom I personally agreed, though maybe not for the same stated reason) thought the seat should be on the same level as the congregation "because the pastor is human like the rest of us." Both factions held the same unarticulated belief that the use of available space in the placement of the pastor's seat would communicate to ourselves and others a basic attitude toward the ministry of and in that church!

Territoriality is another aspect of proxemics that has an impact upon nonverbal communication in a local church. I remember an elderly woman in a church my family attended who "always" sat in the same seat in the same pew every Sunday. One day the church had a new usher "who didn't know the rules." A new family in town came to worship with us, and he ushered them to "this woman's place." When she arrived a few minutes later, she walked down to her regular seat and just stood there in the aisle and stared at them, until they moved (the usher apologized to them and found them other seats, although I don't remember their ever visiting us again). Worshippers tend to gravitate to the same seats Sunday after Sunday, not unlike students in the classroom, and become irritated when someone else is sitting "in their places." Most of us human beings tend to be territorial animals, a fact that training committees need to share with their ushering staff. A Sunday School teacher of a kindergarten class became quite upset when the kindergarten was moved to another room, even though she had been the teacher for less than five years. That was "her room," her territory, and she was not about to give it up without a fight. She felt impelled to defend it. Possibly, if she had been in on the decision, she would have been "reasoned" out of the territory by realizing the benefits of the move to the kindergarten children (i.e., a swap for some "better territory").

The final aspect of proxemics is "environment." This is a catch-all term for "atmosphere" or overall feeling one receives from an area or space. A few years ago, while visiting us in a city to which we had recently moved, my father-in-law attended church with us. Having worshipped for years in a small wooden church in a northern Minnesota village, upon entering this large stone, brick, and glass sturcture, he slowly and sadly shook his head and uttered, "too large, too cold, too hard." He was used to another environment, one of warm, varnished wood, weathered and worn by the bodies and souls of friends and family. This one was too sterile for him. However, that same city church communicated "home" to many of those who worshipped there, people who would not feel "at home" in some other environment. Personally, I prefer heavy wooden beams and glass that opens a congregation to the world into which they are sent. However, when I spent a few months in northern England, I appreciated the ancient cathedrals and country churches made of massive stone pillars and stained windows. I found that environment, also, very conducive to worship. One's worshiping environment does speak a message, a fact that building committees need always be aware.

Paralanguage is the third basic category of nonverbal communication. This term refers to the way our words are spoken, the manner in which they are communicated. Emphasis, tone of voice, pace, pitch, volume, all are part of paralanguage. Reactions of a listener or audience to paralanguage are usually on the feeling level, below the level of consciousness. These reactions are often difficult to analyze or describe: "I don't know. . .It's just the way you said it. . .It isn't what you said that bothers me, it's how you said it." The adult who still has not outgrown the rebellion towards an assertive parental authority figure will probably react negatively towards a preacher who sounds emphatic and deliberate, even if the theology is quite compatible. Someone who speaks in a rapid-fire manner conveys a different paralinguistic message than one who speaks slowly with many pauses. The speaker who does not adjust voice volume to the room or audience size is usually in communication trouble. Speaking too loudly communicates authority, aggressiveness, certainty, and dogmatism. Speaking too softly will communicate shyness, uncertainty, and weakness. "Audible thinking," adding "er's" and "ah's" and "uh's" between words and phrases, tends to communicate lack of training, ignorance, or unpreparedness.

My voice tone is a middle-range baritone. One Christmas in seminary in a radio-drama, I read the part of Joseph. Some of my peers were very critical, not of the way I read the part, but rather that my voice was not "deep enough" for Joseph. Because of the cultural image we have of Abraham Lincoln, it is difficult to imagine his having a rather high piercing voice; yet that is exactly what he did have, not a deep resonating one like Charlton Heston's. Voice tone communicates a message, and, like all reception of symbols, is interpreted according to the listener's individual experiences and perception. An effective communicator will be aware of the many effects of paralanguage.

Beyond the basic three, there are other miscellaneous categories of nonverbal communication. One is the use of time, definitely a culturally rooted phenomenon, and occasionally a cause of stress, especially so when beginning meetings and/or programs. To some people, eight o'clock means exactly that: eight o'clock. To others, it may mean 8:10 or 8:15, depending on when everyone gets there. This latter attitude seems to be the more generally accepted American perception of start-up time for meetings. The Latin American perception of "punctuality" is more like "within an hour or two." The American Indian arrives when it is "appropriate," as I learned when scheduling a speaker in a Human Relations Class I once taught. He had been scheduled to speak at 6:00 PM on a certain Tuesday, but that date and time came and went; still no Steve Greencrow. On the next Tuesday, when another speaker had been scheduled, Steve arrived. His explanation: It was no misunderstanding. It was not appropriate for him to come last Tuesday. We were on "white man's time." He lived on "Indian time." Steve taught me a valuable lesson. Lest we think ourselves "superior" in our use of time, we might consider the frustration of a Swiss businessman who attended one of my courses on Interpersonal Communication in Business. Karl expressed this deep frustration when we were discussing the different concepts of time human beings hold, when he related how Americans misuse time. When a meeting is called for two o'clock, the meeting should start at that time, he argued, whether or not anyone else is present. No wonder we hold "Swiss movement" in such high repute!

When a worship service is scheduled for 11:00 AM, what time do we begin? When the acolyte arrives? When the choir is ready? When the pastor finishes conversing with the usher? Promptness or lack of it will send a message, however significant or not, to the congregation and to any visitors present. How long is the service of worship? Does it end before the hour is over? We Americans seem to be inculturated by radio and television to quarter, half, and full hour segments. More than an hour for almost any activity, including worship, seems to irritate more than a few people in the congregation. Gone are the days when a religious service can take two or three hours, no matter how important the occasion. This is especially true when considering the length of the sermon. Whereas some "more primitive" cultures cannot imagine anything important being expressed in less than an hour, I've heard laypeople repeat over and over again the new adage, "If something can't be said in less than fifteen minutes, it's not worth saying!" An occasional "longer sermon" may be reluctantly accepted by many a congregation today, but not if it becomes a habit.

Body adornment, including clothing, is another category of nonverbal communication. Shakespeare once said "the apparel oft proclaims the man." I think it was Washington Irving who extended this thought to "Clothes make the man."

And we should update this maxim to read "and the woman, too." Some people, both males and females, spend long minutes each morning gazing into their closets deciding what to wear that day. Why? Because what we wear *does* convey a message; else we would throw on any old thing, whether it be color-coordinated or not, wrinkled, dirty, the same garments as yesterday, out-of-fashion, or whatever. It wouldn't matter. I think of the Roman Catholic nun of yesteryear. With her habit she proclaimed one message; today, in regular street clothes, she conveys another. The same is true with the priest and his clerical collar; he just doesn't seem like a priest without it! In my younger days in the pastorate I wore the clerical collar as a Protestant minister. Later on I discarded it as streetwear, and wore it only with my robe during services and on hospital visitations. It was in the hospitals when the message of the collar was the strongest; sometimes without it I was not welcome after visiting hours; I was always welcome anywhere in the hospital when my clerical garb conveyed the message to others: "clergy!" One time I was driving through downtown Montreal with my station wagon full of teenagers who were having a great time distracting me. Suddenly I was traveling the wrong way on a one way street, and a police officer stopped me ready to "ream me out," when he noticed my clerical collar. His frown changed to a smile, his voice softened, he stopped traffic giving me an

113

opportunity to turn around, and he sent me on my way with apologies to me for Montreal traffic patterns. The collar sent a definite nonverbal message.

If a pastor wears a cross or another kind of pendant around the neck, in a liturgical setting or out of it, that, too, sends a message to an observor. The same is true of a pulpit robe or other vestments. I recall one pastor with a PhD in Literature who wore his academic hood in the pulpit on all liturgical occasions. That conveyed a message to his people. A regular business suit with white shirt and "power tie" also speaks a message to a congregation, as does being in shirt sleeves on a hot summer day. Wearing a mustache or beard (as illustrated in Chapter Three) or what is perceived as heavy makeup will communicate a message to the audience. Wear jeans and a flannel shirt when making a hospital call or attending the Women's Group luncheon and see whether or not what we wear on our bodies transmits a message to the people of our parish. The pastor who is aware of this will be a more effective communicator.

Related to the clothing and body adornment category of nonverbal communication is the "attractiveness" phenomenon. Numerous studies have been made which indicate that we human beings tend to associate attractiveness with "worthiness," "intelligence," "leadership," and other more positive attributes, and we relate accordingly.

This human tendency is probably why many people in our society spend so much time, money, and energy on decorating their bodies: to make themselves more attractive, and therefore more appealing and worthy to others. Tallness, in our culture, is perceived as a positive attribute, and taller people, being more "attractive," have an advantage when it comes to vying for leadership. The shorter person can overcome it, certainly, but must work harder and *prove* greater capability. The elementary school child, bathed with clean clothes and combed hair, will be considered more intelligent and responsive by the teacher. The young single mother who comes to the church seeking assistance will be more likely to receive it if she, though obviously poverty stricken, has her hair combed and her clothes hanging straight. Church people or not, we do seem to relate more positively and more benevolently to those needy who are at least somewhat attractive to us. Even in commercial establishments, where selling is the primary objective, the more attractive customer is invariably waited on before the less attractive one. Maybe pastors in their personal behavior can be more aware of this phenomenon and less tempted to discriminate on the basis of personal attractiveness, for surely the "ugly" are worthy, too!

The final miscellaneous category of nonverbal communication is "color," be it the color of one's clothing, a room, a plant, carpet, or whatever.

Cultures have taught their members to respond in certain ways to specific colors. Westerners "see red," the color of passion or anger or excitement. We occasionally "feel blue," the color of light depression, meloncholy, or longing. Black is the color of mourning, of death, of the unknown. We are taught that white symbolizes cleanliness and purity. Stoles and liturgical paraments reflect the messages of color: green for growth; purple for passion; red for vitality and life; black for mourning; white for purity and special celebration. Some Westerners find it difficult to believe that some Chinese cultures, for example, infuse white with the meaning of death and black with celebration.

A Building Committee decision often fraught with tension is on the color of the chancel carpet. Red for life? Green for growth? Blue for color coordination? Brown so it won't look dirty? These are real concerns and hard questions, and verbally minimizing them will only "drive them underground" to emerge in some other form later. What color shall we paint the pastor's study? Pastel blue or green to calm anxiety? Yellow to raise spirits? An off-white to neutralize all emotion and/ or to make the pastor's oak-framed credentials more visible? Color, as a vehicle of nonverbal communication, does hold meaning, influence moods, and transmit messages.

It is impossible to teach someone to communicate nonverbally; we have always known how to do it. We do it naturally. From the warmth and affection inherent in the infant's nuzzling at the mother's breast, to the smile that transforms our face when elated, to the tear that expresses sadness, to the white knuckles on the speaker's stand, to the embrace of affection, to the choice of a day's clothing, to the response to the colors of our environment, we are involved in nonverbal communication. It is culturally natural, something that is learned by living. My only hope is that this lengthy discussion has helped the pastor gain a greater awareness of nonverbal communication and its effect on messages and relationships, and that by understanding this more clearly the pastor may make any necessary adjustments in attitude and behavior toward the goal of a more effective ministry.

Chapter Six
"Be Still and Know"—Some Words About Listening

Then Job answered: If you would only keep silent, that
would be your wisdom! Hear now my reasoning, and
listen to the pleadings of my lips. . Listen carefully to
my words, and let my declaration be in your ears. . .
Listen carefully to my words, and let this be your
consolation. Bear with me, and I will speak, and after I
have spoken, mock on. . .Look at me, and be appalled,
and lay your hand upon your mouth. . .
   And Elihu answered: See, I waited for your words, I
listened for your wise sayings, while you searched out
what to say. I gave you my attention. . Pay heed, Job,
listen to me; be silent, and I will speak. If you have
anything to say, answer me; speak, for I desire to justify
you. If not, listen to me; be silent, and I will teach you
wisdom.
         Job 13:5,6,17;21:2,3,5;32:11,12a;33:31-33 NRSV

    The Book of Job has many such pleas for others
to listen. There is much pain here, and out of the
pain an urgency to be confirmed by another person,
a confirmation that can only come from listening.
If any communication skill is imbued with healing
powers, it must be the skill of listening.

    Many of us pastors were first and most strongly
attracted to the ministry through the power and

influence of the publicly spoken word. We recognized how pastors were able to influence their people through talking. Congregations listened as their pastor spoke. Today many clergy seem not to have moved beyond that; their understood role is to *speak*— out of their knowledge of scripture and theology, out of their experience in working with people, and out of their continuing prayerful and special relationship with God. As we observed in our more impressionable years, members of the assembled congregation assume the role of listeners, to hear the pastor speak the Word of God and reasonably apply it to their lives. Unfortunately a goodly number of pastors, therefore, have never developed the skill of listening. They're so involved in the talking aspect of communicating that listening has little priority in their relationships. I'm convinced that many simply do not know how to listen anymore, if indeed they ever did, and I believe our ministry is the poorer for it.

I am not suggesting that we pastors do not listen for God's Word, either through prayer or through the insights of Scripture. Most of us have learned through experience of the the power of prayer. We have listened for God to speak, and we have not been disappointed. The words of the psalmist in the New Year Festival hymn (Psalm 46), "Be still and know that I am God," is within the experience of us all. Many of us, when we have listened, have heard that same "still small voice" that Elijah heard so many years ago (I Kings 19:12). The noise of the wind, the earthquake, and the fire cannot forever drown out that "voice," when we really listen. Neither can the bursting bomb, the blaring boombox, or the babbling buffoon. God's Voice can be heard, *if* and *when* we listen.

I *am* suggesting that many of us pastors have not adequately applied those listening skills employed at prayertime to relationships we have with our parishoners. Some of us indeed may be overconcentrating on "telling" because we believe we are more knowledgeable on the subject at hand. Others of us may be into "telling" because we believe that is what's expected of us in our roles as leaders in the community. With some, I hope not very many, such behavior may be part of their theological understanding: that through prayer and the reading of Scripture, they believe God gives us pastors all we need to know in order to live a life of faith, and ordinary laypeople do not add to it (i.e., God does not speak to us through them, only through the words of the Bible, the pastor's prayer life, and an occasional bolt of lightning). Whatever the reason(s), listening to people does not seem to have a particularly high priority in the lives of many of us. This is not to say that the pastor who spends a great amount of time in pastoral counseling doesn't listen. It *is* to say that apart from that function, in which we are forced to listen (or to "fake it"), many of us as pastors are not perceived, by our laypeople

121

or by the community at large, as very proficient listeners. Our general image is one of a "teller" and a "talker," rather than a listener.

The above conclusion stands in stark contrast to the findings of most communication researchers (Wolvin, Nichols, Steil, Rankin, Barker, etc.). They discovered that the most important communication skill both on-the-job and in family and social settings was listening. This was as perceived not by the surveyors, but by common everyday ordinary people like those in our churches. If listening is so very important in all other aspects of people's lives, it seems to me that it should be considered of utmost importance in the pastoral ministry as well.

Add to the discussion the fact that 53-63% (depending upon the survey) of the average person's time is spent in situations and relationships with a high incidence of listening possibility. I would imagine that the possibilities for listening in a pastoral role are even somewhat higher. If we would count up all the minutes in a day that we *could* be listening (or *should* be?), the time would at least equal that of other vocations, and probably considerably exceed them.

At this point it would seem worthwhile to correct a few misconceptions about listening, the first being the confusion between "listening" and "hearing." As the reader has without doubt noted already, I do not consider them as synonymns. "Yes, I hear you" is not the same as "I'm listening to you." Many a cartoon has poked fun at this difference, as the stereotypical husband is buried behind his newspaper while his wife harangues him with "Are you listening to me?" Of course, he is hearing, because he answers, or at least grunts; however, we know he is not listening.

The second misconception is related to the first. Listening often is assumed to be a natural behavior, a skill with which we're born. Except where there's a physical handicap, through injury or genetics, *hearing* is the natural ability. *Listening* is a skill to be developed, to be learned.

A third common misconception is that all listeners (or hearers) receive the same message. Nothing could be further from the truth, as we discussed at length in both chapters One and Three. Both hearing and listening are "sorting out" processes in which the receiver of the message gleans meaning from the words and behaviors according to the receiver's ability, motivation, and experience (perception). This sorting out process is rarely the same from individual to individual. All hearers do not receive the same message. Listening skills, when properly developed, can reduce the number of garbled, mixed and misconstrued messages.

A fourth common misconception is that listening and talking are two very different skills; that is, that talking is the antithesis of listening. Not so. Skilled listening *includes the response* one gives to the primary source. I'm referring here, of course, to "feedback," whether it is verbal or nonverbal. Part of the listening skill is the selection of appropriate feedback that will stimulate the speaker to continue communicating and/or to be satisfied that listening has taken place.

There are a number of barriers to listening, some more obvious than others. Physically-based hearing problems create much anxiety in the accurate sending and receiving of messages. As people grow older, this problem more often manifests itself. The physical apparatus in many people simply does not function as well as it once did. Those with a hearing problem are forced to "fill in" what they do not catch, and in "filling in" from their own experience often do not understand accurately. Sometimes they become so frustrated they simply "fake it," and more and more become left out of conversations since they don't bother letting the other conversants know that they're not keeping up with the conversation. The one without the hearing problem assumes the other person has heard—unless something is said to the contrary. When speaking with a person with a hearing problem, the pastor (and anyone else for that matter) should constantly seek feedback as to whether one is being heard or not, and not communicate frustration or an urgency to move on to another point, idea, or conversation. A diminished ability to hear, and therefore to listen as well, has a direct and usually negative effect on the self-concept, and then the barrier will be at least twice as difficult to overcome.

Another barrier to listening is an outgrowth of our modern age. Marshall McLuhan labeled it "information overload." There is so much to hear, to absorb, to make sense of, in our modern world that the human capacity, at least psychologically, seems to be at the outer limits of its stretching point. Many of us yearn for the simpler life with fewer facts to absorb, fewer numbers to memorize, fewer problems to solve, fewer people to see and know, fewer activities in which to be involved, less information to understand. We do seem to be in an age of information overload. As human beings often do as a survival tactic, we just stop hearing; we refuse to listen anymore. Enough is enough.

A third barrier to listening is built into the human brain: we think faster than we speak. As Ralph Nichols, the "granddaddy of listening research," and others have discovered, the brain is capable of translating sounds into meaning at the rate of 600 words per minute; however, the average person speaks only 100 to 140 words per minute. This means that we have considerable "spare time" to think about other things while someone is talking to us. We are tempted to use this "extra" time to daydream, to plan our next statement, to concentrate on noises outside the immediate relationship. Often, when we catch our minds wandering and then return to the conversation, we have missed something important.

A fourth barrier to listening is the internal noise we allow to interfere with the intended message. Each one of us has concerns, problems, dreams, and responsibilities on which we occasionally ponder. These thoughts, which emerge from our own needs and desires, "pop into consciousness" whenever we hear or see something that prompts them to do so, and these thoughts tend to crowd out the message which is being sent to us. Being overtired sometimes becomes an internal noise which evolves into a mood-barrier which in turn becomes a filter through which a message must travel, and because of which will tend to distort the meaning. A busy schedule and time pressure can create so much internal noise that a pastor hears little and listens to practically nothing.

I will label the final barrier to be discussed here, "external distractions." These are the more obvious barriers. The illustration about making a pastoral call in Chapter One is applicable here, too. A blaring television, a child demanding attention, a ringing telephone, all are external distractions ("noise") which diminish listening effectiveness. An ash at the end of a cigarette can be very distracting, expecially when it increases in length as the conversation continues. Conversing in a busy restaurant is not the most conducive to attentive listening, and demands real concentration. There are times when a pastor must meet in these situations and circumstances, as I remember doing occasionally when taking alcoholics through their fifth step, but it involves hard work and constant and conscious "screening-out" of the many intruding distractions.

Beyond these barriers to effective listening which must be surmounted are the many poor listening habits many of us have developed. Adler and Towne, again in their much-referred-to text on interpersonal communication, Looking Out, Looking In, list eight such habits: pseudolistening, stage hogging, selective listening, filling in gaps, insulated listening, defensive listening, insensitive listening, and ambushing. Let's look at these poor listening habits one at a time.

Pseudolistening is an expertise many of us have. In fact, it's a poor listening habit that we hone more sharply each year of our lives, beginning at home during family conversations when we pretend we are listening to Mom or Dad when we're really not, and throughout our school years when we sit in class feigning attention to the teacher. Pseudolistening is that behavior we do when we know we *should* be listening, but *instead* think about something else than what is being said to us. It is the smile on our face, the nod of our head, even a question now and then to keep the other person talking, when our mind is wandering beyond the immediate relationship. It is communicating to the speaker that we are listening when we are really not listening. It is what many people do in the congregation when we are preaching. It is what we pastors sometimes do when we're on a tight schedule and "can't afford" to get into a conversation which will put us further behind.

Stage hogging is an attempt at control. It is keeping attention focused on oneself. Stage hogs don't really care about what others have to say; they are only concerned with expressing themselves. Every now and then, they will allow the other to say something, but it is usually only to catch their own breath or to plan their next statement or to fulfill a need to appear somewhat polite. A stage hog is more into making speeches than into gaining something from a conversational partner. A stage hog is someone who attempts to get a personal agenda covered at almost any cost. Of course, stage-hogging is not unknown in the pastoral ranks, and they usually have their reward: we avoid them whenever possible.

A third poor listening habit is selective listening, reacting and responding only to parts of the other's speaking, the parts that interest us. We ignore anything that doesn't pique our interest, no matter how important that point or subject is to the other person. Selective listening is a highly sophisticated application of our perceptual powers to conversation. We allow into the responsive parts of our brains only those sounds which symbolize a personal concern or interest, and we screen out all others. For example, the person who has a very negative view of life will only hear the bad things which are occurring in the church and world, only immorality, violence and sin, and screen out of consciousness anything that might be considered good or positive, not unlike a criticism many of us have on contemporary media practices. Someone may be so "into" the past that s/he only hears what can be tied easily into what has happened in bygone days, and does not respond to future possibilities. Some people may be so "sportsminded" that they only listen for references to subjects connected in some way to the sportsworld, bringing back into primary conversational focus her/his experience and interest in sports. Others do this with their interest in hermaneutics, television, sex, church politics, or whatever.

Filling-in-gaps is the manufacturing of information in the remembering process. Not hearing everything that is said (for whatever reason), in order to make sense out of the whole story, the "fill-in-gapper" will insert any necessary information. Of course, the manufactured facts and inferences come from the listener's own experience, not the speaker's, thus increasing the probability of distortion. When the story is repeated, either during that conversation or later retold to someone else, the gaps are filled in and the story sounds complete and accurate. It makes sense. However, a response often heard by the original storyteller is "I never said that!"

The fifth poor listening habit is called insulated listening, the opposite of selective listening. Whenever the conversation turns to a subject insulated listeners don't want to discuss, they simply fail to acknowledge it, or, if they're exceptionally skillful, steer the conversation to another more comfortable subject. I've found many an insulated listener among heavy users of alcoholic beverages and other drugs; they either do not hear about their problem, or they simply nod, answer what they know will please, and promptly forget what has been said. I've also known one or two clergypersons who employ insulated listening when their ministerial behavior is being reviewed by either their own laypeople or their ecclesiastical peers: when comments are perceived to be negative, they simply don't hear what is being said.

Defensive listening has been called the "teenager's disease." Unfortunately, it not limited to adolescents. Defensive listeners translate innocent comments on sensitive subjects into personal attacks. When someone, out of simple curiosity, asks "Why did you do it this way?," these people act as if they are being personally challenged, and react with rationalizing, being apathetic, counterattacking, or any one of the many other defensive behaviors. Of course, sometimes an attack is really being made, and defensiveness may be appropriate, but the defensive listener is one who makes a habit of this, seeing far too many comments as personal attacks, when indeed they are not. Some parents fall into this category when their children question a decision and they take it as a challenge to their authority. Clergy sometimes act this same way when one of their decisions is questioned. Most of us will be defensive listeners sometime during our lives, but we should be wary of it becoming habitual.

Insensitive listening is the poor listening habit which hears the words being spoken, but ignores the nonverbal messages being sent. Insensitive listeners do not look behind the words to the hidden messages which are sometimes present. Taking words at face value but not seeing the tear in the speaker's eye or hearing the quavering in the voice, is an example of insensitivity. Since the appropriateness of listening behavior is contextual, it would be unwise for a pastor to look for a hidden or subtle message in every comment made. However, many an opportunity for ministering has been lost by a pastor's insensitive listening, and many a ministry has been less effective than it could have been as a result of habitual insensitive listening.

The last poor listening habit I'll identify is called ambushing. Ambushers listen carefully enough to collect information with which to attack the other person. These are people who focus on winning as their goal, even when there is no contest existing. They seem to have a psychological need to be better than the other person, and they attempt to achieve this by showing the other person as wrong or misled or misinformed by "tripping them up" with the specific information collected just for that purpose—information collected from the speaker's own statements. I wish that no one in our world would ever employ such a poor listening habit, but I know there are people like this, and even in some of the churches we serve. The clergy has not been totally devoid of ambushers, either.

People who do not or will not listen have some justification for not doing so: listening opens up the listener to possible change. If we do not listen to someone, we do not need to worry about hearing a differing point of view, therefore receiving no new information upon which to base any change in our thinking. Not listening is a defense against change. In the "unpacking" part of a listening exercise I often did in class ("unpacking" being the discussion that follows the exercise per se), an exercise in which students with opposing points of view are paired for discussion on a topic, the most frequent reaction reported is that it is very difficult to listen to the other side, and when they do listen, they often are forced to modify their own point of view. People of all ages and in all walks of life seem to sense this danger inherently, hence often shy away from listening to someone holding a perceived different point of view. However, growth can only occur as new information and perceptions are made available to us. Conclusion: no listening, no growth.

It should be acknowledged here: the goal of all listening behavior is not the same. Sometimes we listen to gain information (as in an academic/ workshop setting or to hear the perception of someone with whom we are conversing). Sometimes we listen to another person in order to help that person handle some problem. The pastor, in the course of the ministry, will do both. Each goal takes a slightly different set of skills. Listening to gain new information will include assimilating facts and inferences by associating them with already understood information, attending primarily to words and ideas, grouping and categorizing concepts for easier recall, asking questions to reduce confusion and to seek additional information, and critically evaluating what is said for its logic and intellectual veracity. I will not elaborate further on this kind of listening behavior, only suggest to the reader that s/he read one of the many helpful books on the subject. My concern is to look more closely at "listening to help," a responsibility which pastors are frequently called upon to fulfill as part of their ministry.

There are six major styles of "listening to help" (Adler and Towne, Looking Out, Looking In, 6th ed.): one I would never recommend; two, occasionally; and two, infrequently. Only one style produces positive results enough to recommend it consistently. The first of the problematical styles is called *advising.* The image many of us pastors project to our congregations is that of an "advice-giver." People come to us to get their problems solved through the advice we give them. Unfortunately, giving advice seldom has more than short-range benefit, if any benefit at all. I remember as a youth hearing what I was told to be an old American Indian adage: "Don't judge another person until you have walked in his moccasins for two moons." This is equally valid when tempted to offer advice as a pastor: "Since you have not walked in another's moccasins at all, it is unwise to offer that person advice on how to do so." Even that "If I were you" phrase is inappropriate, because I am not you. In addition to this obvious concern is another: when we offer advice as to how to solve a problem and the other person takes our advice, but our solution doesn't work, s/he will often shift the blame for its not working onto us, thereby not taking responsibility for her/his own actions, as needed for healthy growth.

Another image under which some of us pastors labor is that of *a judge.* Some of us are perceived as people who are ready to judge another person for problematical behavior. Only people who enjoy their guilt and the perceived judgment it brings will come to a pastor who exhibits this kind of listening behavior. Most people steer clear of such "listeners."

Hearing "shame on you," or some form of it, as some of us did as youngsters, is not a pleasant experience, and seldom makes people feel accepted and loved. Even hearing "that's good" over and over again, as some people overuse positive reinforcement, is a judging response which can make people so dependent on it that its absence is perceived as judgment.

A third style of listening-to-help is the *analytical* style. This is similar to the lay-perception of psycholanalysis, the picking-apart of the psyche and putting it back together again in a more effective way. Few of us are trained sufficiently to do this, and sometimes we do far more harm than good. Once in a while an analytical statement such as "I think I know what is really bothering you is..." or a "Maybe the problem started when..." will produce helpful results; however, we pastors need to be careful in using this style very often since our interpretation may not be at all correct and therefore confusing or misleading, or such an interpretation may cause undue defensiveness on the part of the person who needs to talk. We pastors need to know our limitations in employing this kind of listening behavior.

The fourth style of listening-to-help, for want of a better word, is called *supporting.* It is a style that emerges from the positive motivation of wanting to affirm the other person; however, it sends mixed messages. "You'll feel better in the morning" (supporting mixed with implied advising), or "It's not as bad as you may think" (supporting mixed with a bit of judgment), or "You really don't have anything to worry about, you'll do a great job" (supporting with some judgment thrown in), are examples of this style, which, while affirming the person, tend to denigrate the problem as a real one, thereby disconfirming the person at the same time by denying the importance of the person's concern. Certainly there are times when encouragement is important; however, supportive listening is infrequently the way to do it, and the wise communicator will avoid its habitual use.

The last, and probably least problematical of the five less-than-satisfactory styles of listening when attempting to help someone is *questionning.* As a way of bringing into the conversation more information which might shed light on the problem at hand, questionning may be helpful. However, it is not without its drawbacks, too. Sometimes the line of questionning can be perceived as snooping into private affairs, and therefore lead to a reduction of self-disclosure. Sometimes we ask questions about some aspect of the problem that is really little else than curiosity on our part and has nothing to do with the real issue. Sometimes the questions we ask only lead the other person on a wild goose chase, a needless exploration of a dead-end street and a time-waster, rather than to a helpful solution. Appropriate and helpful questionning is a style of listening that needs to be carefully applied and takes time and experience to develop.

The one consistently more-positive-than-negative style of listening-to-help is known by different names. Some call it "active listening;" some call it "reflective listening;" some call it "listening for understanding;" others, "dialogical listening;" others, "confirmational listening;" still others, "therapeutic listening." I have my own pet name: "*relational listening.*" However, all of these labels point to the same goal of listening-to-help, which seems to me primarily a matter of emphasis, and any of these names is adequate for our purpose in this chapter. Because I am writing this book, I'll use my own pet label, "relational listening."

The first element in this style of listening is the attempt to reduce distractions to the lowest possible level. The focus should be on the person speaking; interruptions should be kept at a minimum, if not eliminated altogether. For the listener, in those few moments, the world consists of that relationship, and that relationship alone. The next appointment is a world away. The busy schedule in the head should be forgotten for those moments.

The second element in relational listening is the attempt to avoid any pre-judging. The listener is hearing what may be an old problem from a new person, making this a new concern for which old answers probably will not satisfy; therefore, pre-judging would be counterproductive. Even if the listener does know "what is best," it is wise not to make that judgment for reasons elaborated earlier in this chapter. Since pre-judging is a form of collective labeling (being prejudiced), it is antithetical to the individual relationship of the moment.

Flexible paraphrasing is the primary responding-skill in relational listening. This is the frequent attempt at reflecting back to the speaker the messages that are received, both the verbal and the nonverbal message. This is done for two reasons: 1) to check out with the speaker if the message received is the message intended; and 2) to allow the speaker to hear what is being said as if s/he were the listener and not the message source, in a sense "objectifying" the concern. The first reason has as its purpose to understand, and to communicate to the speaker that s/he is being understood. This is extremely important; we want to be understood, but we also *need to know* we're being understood. This knowledge alone is strong medicine and offers some immediate relief to a struggling soul in need of some way to overcome the aloneness that often comes with a weighty burden.

In its most elementary form, an example of flexible paraphrasing might be, "I'm hearing you say, through your words and through the edge in your voice, that you are very frustrated and have probably reached the limit on what you're going to take from her, that if she doesn't stop this behavior soon, you're going to ask her to leave. Is this what you meant to tell me?" This simplified, non-mechanical, unstructured, non-formalized response both checks with the speaker to see if the message received is the same message that was intended, and it gives the speaker an opportunity to hear what s/he said in order to view it more objectively. From this less subjective hearing, the speaker is better able to sort out the thoughts and feelings and, in doing so, be in a better position to solve her/his own problems in a more competent manner.

If a pastor is to become a more effective listener, there are four basic attitudes which must be taken into any listening situation. The first has to do with motivation. The pastor must *want* to listen. This is not something that only requires a half-hearted effort. Sometimes we become too busy or preoccupied to help someone, and that's understandable. However, if that is the case, to pretend attention, to feign concern helps no one. In fact, it just may do irreparable harm to the relationship. If you don't really want to be involved in relational listening, don't. The lack of motivation will be spotted (and resented) sooner or later, or you will become so exhausted from long, intensive playacting that it will take its toll on your own health and abilities.

The second basic attitude is a willingness to take

the necessary time to listen relationally. Therapeutic listening takes time, lots of time. It is not something that can be done quickly. The checking out process and the act of giving quality feedback and the waiting for the speaker to discover the solution bit by bit, all takes time. If the pastor doesn't have, or won't take the necessary time, relational listening is impossible. Of course, there are certain people who insist on being time-wasters, and there are situations in which the conversation must be limited by time constraints. Admittedly, such conversations need to be brought to a conclusion, and such situations need to be handled diplomatically. However, if the listener communicates in any way to the speaker that time for listening is either scarce or unavailable, at the present moment or in the near future, the opportunity for relational listening may well quickly disappear.

The third basic attitude necessary for listening relationally is the willingness to keep attention focused on the problem-holder. Even if the listener believes her/his own experiences are more interesting and/or enlightening, and therefore might like to share them just for the joy of sharing them, to do so would be departing from this style of listening. Sometimes, in the act of listening, the pastor might have cause to become defensive, perceiving a personal attack; however, this should be avoided, for defending oneself shifts the focus away from the problem at hand and away from the problem-holder. Because of the high energy that focusing expends, relational listening is exhausting business, and should not be employed in every conversation lest "burn-out" easily occur.

The fourth and final basic attitude necessary for relational listening is acceptance of the other person and that person's point of view. This does not mean the pastor must be in agreement with the speaker, nor that the pastor should modify her/his own beliefs to accommodate the other. It does mean the pastor should accept the other person as a human being worthy of a relationship, and should accept the speaker's concern as a valid one, springing from the speaker's own experience as self-interpreted. In fostering this atmosphere of acceptance, the pastor should resist imposing her/his own ideas on the speaker, trusting that person to discover any new insights and solutions. Because the relational listener trusts the other in this manner, moralizing, manipulating, or any other attempts at forcing change on the other person are inappropriate, and would likely be perceived as an attempt to demean, once suspected.

The most important benefit of effective listening, be it relational listening in a helping situation, or only to hear someone else's point of view in a friendly conversation, is that it affirms the speaker. Effective listening communicates "You are important to me and worthy of my attention," a message dearly needed by all of us. It seems to me that this is near the core of the gospel, not unlike the message of God to human beings, that we are important to God and worthy of God's attention. As representatives of God, as persons made in God's image, we have within our power to affirm people as worthy by giving them our attention in the act of listening. Whatever we might think of Elihu's theology, there is one attitude we need to emulate more often in our ministry: "I gave you my attention."

Chapter Seven
Self-Disclosing

> My God, my God, why have you forsaken me? Why are
> you so far from helping me, from the words of my
> groaning? O my God, I cry by day, but you do not
> answer; and by night, but find no rest. . . I am a worm,
> and not human; scorned by others, and despised by
> the people. All who see me mock at me; they make
> mouths at me, they shake their heads;. . . I am poured
> out like water, and all my bones are out of joint; my
> heart is like wax; it is melted within my breast; my
> mouth is dried up like a potsherd, and my tongue sticks
> to my jaws; you lay me in the dust of death. For dogs
> are all around me; a company of evildoers encircles me.
> My hands and feet have shriveled... I can count all my
> bones. They stare and gloat over me.
> Psalm 22:1,2,6,7,14-17 NRSV

The Psalmist here is opening himself to God, expressing his innermost feelings, sharing his hurt, his frustration, his anger, his confusion, his righteous indignation. He is self-disclosing. When Jesus hung upon the cross, nearing the end of his pain and his life, he cried out to God with those same words, remembering the Psalmist's anguish, "My God, my God! Why have you forsaken me?" Jesus, too, was self-disclosing. Those feelings of the moment were being expressed. He was telling

Another how he felt.

Unfortunately, self-disclosing has another commonly-held definition. Many seem to think it is nothing else but telling someone the deep, dark, dirty secrets of the past. As I told my students, that is not self-disclosing; that is stupidity. Such behavior does more harm than good to a relationship. The skill of self-disclosing, and it is a communication skill, is telling another person how you feel, what you are thinking, what you are sensing, what you want, what you are doing *at this particular moment.* Past feelings, thoughts, desires, and actions are relevant *only* as they shed light on the present relationship and situation, therefore those secrets we all have and of which we are so ashamed and which give rise to all those guilt feelings really have no place in self-disclosure. However, the present *feelings* we have about them may very well be part of the present relationship. Disclosing them in this context is well within our definition. Besides the primary benefits of *doing* self-disclosure, as I'll be discussing at greater length, simply *understanding* what the skill is and how it works can help a person sort through the differences between past behaviors and present thoughts and feelings, a commendable goal in and of itself.

Most people hold deep fears about self-disclosing. It is frightening to do so, especially if the trust level is not comfortably secure. In his book, <u>Soul on Ice</u>, Eldridge Cleaver vividly describes this fear in words with which most of us can identify:

> Getting to know someone, entering that new world, is an ultimate, irretrievable leap into the unknown. The prospect is terrifying. The stakes are high. The emotions are overwhelming. The two people are reluctant really to strip themselves naked in front of each other, because in doing so they make themselves vulnerable and give enormous power over themselves one to the other. How often they inflict pain and torment upon each other. Better to maintain shallow, superficial affairs; that way the scars are not too deep. No blood is hacked from the soul.

Not only does the fear of making oneself vulnerable cause people to resist self-disclosing, but also certain cultural teachings which reinforce this fear. Three common examples: it's a sign of egotism to talk about oneself; it's immature and inappropriate to express emotion; and it's a sign of weakness not to handle problems by oneself. Some ethnic families do communicate that it's acceptable to express sadness; however, these same families may communicate down through the years that it is not acceptable to express a feeling of pride in one's own accomplishments, lest others think ill of their "bragging." All sorts of combinations of cultural teachings exist to support our natural fear of self-disclosing, and pastors are wise to know the prevailing lessons which are taught in their parishes regarding the behavior of self-disclosing.

John Powell, in his near-classic little book, <u>Why Am I Afraid To Tell You Who I Am?</u>, also describes our fear very succinctly: "I am afraid to tell you who I am, because, if I tell you who I am, you may not like who I am, and that's all I have." In another of his books, <u>The Secret of Staying in Love</u>, Powell describes forty-eight topics which, if discussed by two people in a dyadic relationship, will go a long way both to breaking down the barriers to self-disclosing and to developing a bond of trust which makes self-disclosing much less uncomfortable. I used thirty-six of his topics in a quarter-long assignment in a class I taught on Interpersonal Communication. Partners (dyads) were chosen at random (drawing names from a hat) during the first week of class; people who already knew each other had their names put back in the hat for another drawing—until everyone was paired with someone they did not know or knew very slightly. They were given handouts on which were printed the thirty-six topics, with developed, explanatory, and probing sub-questions for each topic. Each dyad was to meet outside of class once a week and discuss four topics, in order, for nine weeks of the term. Rarely was there a mismatch, people who rubbed each other the wrong way and who simply could not get along with each other. Except for that rarity, the students developed a high and enviable trust level and became fast friends—through a structured process of self-disclosure, though they started out as almost total strangers. I and my students, both traditional-age students and older, non-traditional, discovered that once we overcame our initial resistance to self-disclosing, deeper and more fulfilling relationships became possible.

Besides creating opportunities for new relationships to develop, self-disclosing will usually enhance already established ones. In a class on Interpersonal Communication I taught to nurses and staff at a local hospital, one person dropped the class, leaving an odd number of registrants. (I always insisted on an even number for the sake of pairing for the above-described experience.) In discussing my dilemma with the class, one woman suggested a solution about which I had major reservations; however, no better solution was found, so she would be paired with her husband who was not taking the class. They would go through the same process, self-disclosing bit-by-bit each week on the topics, setting aside time to do so in their daily schedules. It seemed to work quite well, and she wrote a fine summary report on the development of their relationship during the term (part of the overall assignment). Though they had been married for over twenty years, she did not know him very well, she indicated, especially since he was not a person who readily shared his feelings. The quarter ended, reports were returned with my comments, and grades were recorded. I did not see this woman soon thereafter, until running into her in a local retail store rather late at night a month or so after the term had ended. She saw me first, and suddenly she appeared before me with tears streaming down her cheeks. "Bob, I meant to call you before this, but I was afraid I'd break down even more than I am now. I wanted to thank you for that class at the hospital. It did far more good than you'll ever realize! Two weeks ago when I came home from work, my husband was on the floor dead—a heart attack. If it hadn't been for your class and all those topics we discussed together as partners, I wouldn't have known what a wonderful man he really was. We told things to each other that we'd never shared before—thoughts and feelings and hopes and dreams. We really self-disclosed! I wouldn't have known his thoughts about death, nor what kind of a funeral he wanted, but that was one of our topics, so I knew. Talking together during that course and the two weeks later on our own before his death were the best times of my life. And I'll never forget them. And I want to thank you." The act of self-disclosing not only opens the door to meaningful relationships, it also enriches already established relationships, as this young widow discovered.

Of course, self-disclosing is not without its risks. John Powell cited a very real one in the above quotation: self-disclosure might lead to rejection. If the other person doesn't like the part of the self you disclose, or doesn't accept who you've disclosed yourself to be, that's all you have. And that can be devastating. A second risk, related to the first but not exactly the same, is that self-disclosure might create a negative image of the self in the mind of the other person. It might not lead to total rejection, but the other person may not think so highly of you and you could lose that person's respect. A third risk is that self-disclosing might actually hurt the other person, and being kind people, we don't want to take a chance on their being hurt. A fourth risk is that in self-disclosing, once the "secret" is out, you experience a loss of control in the relationship because the other person will interpret the new information according to that person's own perception. And who knows what will result? A fifth risk, and a commonly felt one, especially in affectionate relationships, is that saying how I really feel or what I really think (both aspects of self-disclosing) might be different from what the other person is feeling or thinking, and it could possibly weaken the relationship because our thoughts and feelings may not be the same. All five of these risks are present when self-disclosure is being contemplated. And it is true, any one or combination *could* result. Self-disclosure is risky business!

However, self-disclosure has its essential benefits as well. In fact, the potential benefits are at least as great, if not greater, particularly so if communicated in a skillful manner at an appropriate time. The first benefit is that self-disclosing can make relationships more satisfying, as the widowed nurse discovered in relating to her husband. Numerous recent studies have concluded that the act of self-disclosing more often than not leads to better liking, to less stressful relationships, and to a reduction of ambiguity about each other's intentions. Self-disclosure is positively related to marital satisfaction, even improving troubled marriages when coupled with guidance from a skilled counselor. A second benefit to moderate and skillful self-disclosure is improved mental health. As Sidney Jourard and others have discovered in their research, people who withhold information about themselves (do not self-disclose) actually create stress for themselves as they exert considerable energy in their attempts to keep feelings hidden from significant others. When self-disclosure finally occurs, there is usually a great feeling of relief, as if a weight is lifted from their shoulders. The mental energy exerted in repressing the expression of feelings and ideas can now be directed in more productive and satisfying ways. A third benefit to self-disclosing is increased self-understanding. The act of sharing information about one's own ideas and feelings serves to bring them out into the open light for looking at them more clearly and, in a way, less subjectively. We gain new insights from seeing our ideas and feelings in a new perspective, apart from the quiet recesses of our own minds. Self-understanding is also increased when the other person follows your norm, as very frequently happens, and in reciprocally self-disclosing, reveals more information about you, the subject you are discussing, and whatever feelings s/he has about you and your behavior.

The same risks and benefits exist for pastors in their parishes as for any other group of people. A member of the clergy sometimes imagines s/he has "more to lose" from exposing the self to another, which may or may not be true; but it is equally true that the pastor has more to gain from self-disclosing, too: improved relationships, increased mental health, and deeper self-understanding, all of which add up to a more effective ministry.

People will self-disclose for all sorts of other reasons, beyond desiring to obtain these three benefits (of which they are usually unaware). Sometimes a person will perceive a need for catharsis, a need to "get something off my chest." This could be more the aforementioned "stupidity" than real self-disclosure, especially if it results in nothing more than transferring a burden of guilt from the self to pity or depression on the part of the other. Or it could be the expression of a deep-felt anger whose cathartic effect is only to drive the other person away. Sometimes people realize through experience that their self-disclosure begets self-disclosure from the other person and it is an effective way to get information about them. Then

151

there are times when selective self-disclosure will create desired impressions. We select the information to share that will result in the kind of image we want the other person to have of us. Some people self-disclose frequently in order to clarify their own opinions and beliefs, in a way "talking the problem out" and seeking feedback from others. Some people disclose information about themselves in hope that the listener will reinforce what they have said, seeking validation of one's behavior or point of view. These last two reasons for self-disclosing are often behind occasional to frequent self-references a pastor makes in the sermon: self-clarification and self-validation. Then there are what I call the "less honorable" reasons for self-disclosing: in order to control other people and manipulate their behavior. And there are those few people who have become very adept at disclosing just the right information about themselves that will likely lead the other person into feeling pity, or becoming defensive, or acting inappropriately. Emotions for such people have become weapons of power to be wielded and expressed skillfully in order to determine another person's behavior. Personally, I find myself frequently trying to avoid such people; however, I must realize that they, too, being God's children, are to be "ministered unto" by a caring and ever-so-patient pastor.

Joseph Luft and Harry Ingham, in 1955, created

an interesting and helpful model for looking at self-disclosure. They called it the "Johari Window" (Luft: <u>Group Processes: An Introduction to Group Dynamics</u>). If you could imagine a frame that contains everything possible that could be known about you, then divide that frame into vertical halves, labeling the left half "All that I know about myself" and the right half "All that I do not know about myself," then taking that same frame and dividing it into horizontal halves, labeling the top half "All that others know about me," and the bottom half "All that others do not know about me," you have your Johari Window that divides everything there is to know about you into four parts.

	Known to self	Not known to self
Known to others	1 Open	2 Blind
Not known to others	3 Hidden	4 Unknown

I have also labeled each of the four parts: Open, Blind, Hidden, and Unknown. The Open segment contains all those facts, attitudes, behaviors, etc.

that both you and other people know about you. The Blind segment contains everything others know about you that you do not realize or acknowledge about yourself. The Hidden segment contains all about you that you know but others do not. Lastly is the Unknown segment, which visually admits that no one ever fully knows or understands oneself nor is ever fully understood; it is to acknowledge that we are still growing and changing as individuals, and there is always more to discover about ourselves.

Before we look at the Johari Window as an interactive model, I need to add two more parts:

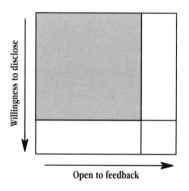

The vertical arrow indicates your willingness to disclose information about yourself. The more willing you are to share your feelings and ideas with others, the larger your "open" quadrant becomes and the smaller your "hidden" quadrant becomes. The horizontal arrow indicates your willingness to listen to feedback about yourself from others, to acknowledge, evaluate, and assimilate their views on you as a person. The more open you are to such feedback, the larger your "open" quadrant is, and the smaller your "blind" quadrant is. If you're both willing to disclose and be open to feedback, your "open" quadrant is very large, with smaller "hidden" and "blind" quadrants, and a minimally-sized "unknown" portion.

The Johari Window becomes even more enlightening when placed next to another one (which, for illustration's sake, is reversed), as representations of two people with differing levels of self-disclosure.

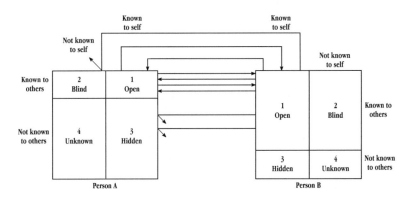

The above arrows show what happens when a more self-disclosing (open) person is in conversation with a less self-disclosing (closed) person. The limited self-disclosure, coupled with less willingness to accept feedback (the two frequently go together), blocks communication. This is a graphic representation of a common communication problem, one that not infrequently finds its way into the pastor's study and cries out for counseling: one person in a relationship is very open with feelings, and shares thoughts and ideas regularly, while the other person doesn't, and both become frustrated. An understanding of this relational tension as a communication problem, as a self-disclosing problem specifically, is sometimes enough to provoke a negotiated change that might lead to a more satisfying relationship. A sharing of the two persons' Johari Windows could be a valuable tool for counseling. And, such graphic knowledge might also help pastors understand some of their own relationships, vocational as well as personal.

Thus far, my focus has been on understanding the concept of self-disclosure, with little, beyond implication, on *how* to self-disclose. The "Star of Introspection" can be of help here. (It is based on the concept and ideas developed by Miller, Nunnally, and Wackman in their <u>Alive and Aware: Improving Communication in Relationships</u>.) Unless we are aware of our own sensing, thoughts, feelings, desires, and actions, we cannot communicate them effectively to others; thus, a "star" (model) to help us identify our own sensations, ideas, emotions, goals, and behaviors. As the "Star" of the New Testament nativity story provided insight for the world, so this "star" can provide insight for an individual.

The first step in the process of employing the "Star" is to use the word "I" as the acknowledged starting point for the sharing of this self-awareness. It is *not* self-disclosing to say, "*You* make me think, or feel, or want, or do," an accusation based upon myth and ignorance; it *is* self-disclosing to say, "*I* think, or feel, or want, or am doing." The second step in the process is to stay with "the here and now." What is important is the present moment, not yesterday or tomorrow. However, as expressed previously, if yesterday or tomorrow is affecting the five points of the "star" *today*, then and only then is it important in self-disclosure. This sharing of the "Star of Introspection" with another person, of course, is what we've been labeling as "self-disclosure."

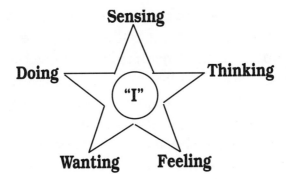

Having the "Star of Introspection" in mind and available as a tool for my own conscious behavior will help me self-disclose without being tempted to divulge those deep, dark, dirty secrets I'm so afraid

157

of revealing. I can relate to another by saying, "I hear an edge to your voice, and I see your fists clenched, and I think I may have angered you, and I feel badly about that. I want to be friends, and I'm trying to apologize." In saying something like this, I have self-disclosed around the Star, hopefully not with an overly-simplified example which communicates a simplistic or non-important conversational skill. Employing the Star of Introspection, either in its totality or one or two parts at a time, as a communication tool, admittedly carries with it all the risks of self-disclosure as discussed above, but it also opens the possibilities for the aforementioned benefits as well.

There exists a helpful tool for informally measuring the depth of a relationship by the kind and intensity of self-disclosing that is occuring between the conversants. It is an identifiable four-level observation. First is the phatic level, the "How are you? I'm fine" exchange, the level which has the least depth. Little real self-disclosing is occuring here, other than expressing a willingness to participate in social niceties. This is often understood as the level at which relationships begin. As someone once described it to me, this is the "grease of social relationships," without which interaction would be poorer indeed. It is talking about the weather, the meal just enjoyed, reiterating the obvious, commenting on an attractive outfit, or making a tentative statement of anticipation regarding some upcoming event of relative inconsequence. This level of interaction is not to be scoffed at as unimportant; rather, it should be seen as a non-threatening acknowledgment of each other's existence and presence. It is an affirmation of a relationship, no matter how momentary or superficial. Phatic communication is a positive response to another person, when the alternative might be ignoring the person or experiencing a mutual embarassment sometimes brought on by silence. Indeed, it may be "social grease," verbalizations which start and/or maintain innumerable conversations; however, phatic communication expresses very little of a self-disclosing nature. It is relatively "safe."

The second level of observable self-disclosing is called "gossip." This is not the commonly held understanding of gossip, meaning "talking about other people's business, usually in a deprecating manner." Gossip, according to our working definition here, is simply "the act of talking about other people." It may be talking about Uncle Joe's operation, or Jim's bout with depression, or Jane's new job, or Tanya and Todd's recent wedding, or Phil's new appointment as pastor in a big city church. Gossip here is conversation about anybody outside the two involved personalities. There is a bit more self-disclosing here than in the phatic level, for it is impossible to mention other people without at least implying some liking or not liking. There is a hint of a relationship, from simple curiosity or passing interest to deep concern or degree of affection. When speaking of a relationship with someone else, however minor it may be, we are self-disclosing, we are reducing that hidden part of ourselves and increasing the open segment (as in the Johari Window). Such talk is a bit more risky than the weather, since we can do something about a relationship, as we have some control over it. This means we must take some responsibility for our curiosity, interest, concern, or affection, and if these marks of relationship are not accepted, approved, or appreciated by the person with whom we are conversing, it could affect the immediate relationship. Thus the degree of risk. Self-disclosing at the level of gossip requires a limited amount of trust.

The third level of observable self-disclosure is called "idea-exchange," and it requires another step up the ladder of trust, for we are opening up our inner self as a repository of ideas to another human being. Our thoughts, the material which makes up our ideas, are our own, and in sharing them, we are exposing our private matter to public view, however limited that is in a single conversation. Once the idea is expressed to another person, it can no longer be denied as being held, and is now subject to evaluation by the other person. It is a fairly deep level of self-disclosure, involving moderate risk and requiring some amount of trust.

The fourth, and deepest level of self-disclosure is called "shared feelings," and, as a category, is itself divided into two parts or levels. For whatever reason, sharing feelings seems to be very difficult for most people in America's dominant culture, as it is in a number of cultures around the world (although not all, by any means). Of the two sub-levels of shared feelings, the less risky is verbally or nonverbally identifying the emotions I am presently feeling. If it is anger, then telling the other person "I am angry; that really bugs me!" or nonverbally showing anger by clenched fists, becoming red in the face, or raising my voice. If it is sadness, then telling the other person "I feel very badly that this happened to him," or nonverbally showing sadness by my voice cracking or by weeping. I am allowing the other person to glimpse inside me and see how something affects me emotionally. This is very risky and requires much trust, for I am opening myself to evaluation at a very deep level. However, the deeper of the shared-feeling sub-levels requires even more trust and carries with it considerable risk. That is telling the other person how I feel about her/him— identifying and sharing those emotions that I hold about the relationship between the person with whom I'm conversing and me. In other words, how do *I* feel about *you*? This is the deepest level of self-disclosing, for I open myself to the possibility of nonreciprocal feelings or even to rejection.

Whatever I say about "us" will affect the immediate relationship, and, once expressed, is out of my control. I am now dependent upon your response. This is why sharing feelings about the immediate relationship is so risky and requires considerable trust.

These four levels (or degrees) of self-disclosure, phatic, gossip, idea-exchange, shared feelings, are observable—in one's own behavior and in the behavior of others. The category in which conversants relate most frequently indicates the amount of risk they are willing to take in the relationship and consequently the degree of trust they have in each other. Such knowledge is very helpful, I have found, in the counseling opportunities of a pastor. It is also helpful in accessing the relationships a pastor has with individual members of the parish. If there is only a willingness to talk about the weather or the local sports scene and a shying away from anything deeper, the parishoner is expressing a low level of trust in the relationship. If the person talks about what John is doing, or about Michelle's upcoming wedding, s/he is self-disclosing to a greater degree and expressing a bit more trust. If the parishoner shares an idea about some phase of church work, a bit higher risk is being taken and more trust expressed. When feelings held enter the conversation, the willingness to risk and to trust becomes more evident, and self-disclosure is at a very deep level. Then, when a person shows a willingness to observably identify feelings about the immediate relationship with you, the pastor, the very deepest level of self-disclosure is occuring, for high risk is being taken and extreme trust is being expressed.

As I have already indicated, self-disclosure is not only expressed verbally. Sometimes we self-disclose by allowing our nonverbal expressions to carry our message. We might "screw up" our face in disgust as a comment on the weather, or open our eyes very wide as a reaction to hearing something about someone else, or nod our head in agreement in response to an idea expressed, or not attempt to hide a tear when viewing a touching scene on television, or embrace someone in greeting or expressing sympathy. These nonverbal behaviors, when *consciously* expressed, are legitimately labeled as self-disclosure. Other nonverbals, when *not* consciously expressed as conveyors of meaning, or when received by another though not intended by the sender, are certainly behaviors of *disclosure*; however, they are not vehicles of *self*-disclosure. When a message received is not meant to be sent, looking at the behavior with the help of the Johari Window, the person is exposing something from the "blind" or "hidden" segment of her/his being. An effective pastor, in being alert for inadvertant disclosure of these areas of a personality, may find unexpected

163

opportunities for ministering.

One common method of avoiding self-disclosure is to tell "a little white lie." Rather than expressing one's real feelings on a subject or about a person or relationship, many people give in to the temptation to lie about it, often under the guise of not wanting to hurt the other person. In all probability, at least in my own experience, the real reason more often is to protect oneself from the consequences of self-disclosing, to eliminate the risk of self-disclosure. "If I tell her what I really think about the meal, she'll think I'm ungrateful and unappreciative." So I tell her the meal was good as usual, or, to "protect" my own integrity (self-image as a non-liar), I'll say something like "It was very tasty, but the company was even better!" She can figure out what I mean by all that. A pastor's little white lies are frequently "on the menu" of many a church potluck supper!

Sidney Jourard in 1971 and others since that time have discovered gender differences in self-disclosing behavior. The earlier conclusion was that women self-disclose much more freely than men; however, that has been somewhat modified in recent years. It seems that self-disclosing differences between the sexes greatly depends on situations, relationships, and inculturation. Women self-disclose less to strangers than do men; they disclose more negative information about themselves; they tend to be more intimate and personal than men. Men, on the other hand, disclose more about their family relationships, interests, and tastes. One interesting finding is that males who perceive themselves as attractive self-disclose more than other males, and females who perceive themselves as attractive disclose less than other females. A consistent conclusion of these studies is that both men and women generally prefer to self-disclose with people of the opposite sex. Satisfaction within family relationships seems to correlate with the kind and amount of self-disclosure family members do (e.g., higher satisfaction, more self-disclosing done), and frequently there is a difference between male and female perception of satifaction. These studies are on the increase, as male-female communication is becoming more and more a field of scholarly interest, and the findings are much more complex than this brief introduction can cover. I do suggest, though, that readers interested in this communication phenomenon investigate the available material (e.g., Jourard, Tannen, Pearson).

An awareness of male-female differences in self-disclosure is important to the pastoral ministry, especially since this once mostly male vocation is increasingly being supplied by females. The differences in self-disclosing behavior and the responses to it by the people of the parish are important to understand in order to reduce the frustration and misunderstanding that can occur in the pastoral relationship. In the dominant American culture, as in many other world cultures, sexual identification does seem to make a difference in self-disclosing behavior, and the wise minister will be aware of it.

My experience, both as a pastor myself and having related to numerous pastors over the years, is that we need to participate in self-disclosure more often. Maybe, with the influx of women into the vocation, the men will be more willing to do so. We seem to be a rather self-protective lot, maybe with good reason; however, we often do miss out on the benefits of self-disclosing. One of our emphases, as counselors, spiritual advisors, and members of a helping vocation, is to encourage others to self-disclose, without focusing on ourselves and our own needs. For some of us, this encouragement of others to self-disclose becomes so much of a focus that we forget the need for balance, and so do not increase the size of *our own* "open" segment, resulting in a larger than is healthy "hidden" segment. As growing communicators, we need to develop greater skill in self-disclosing, if not in our vocational relationships, then at least finding someone with whom we may share some of the "hidden," and hear some of the "blind," thereby reducing the "unknown," and increasing the "open." I'm not suggesting here that we find some "confessor" to hear our sins (although sometimes this may not be such a bad idea!); I am suggesting that we have someone who will hear our ideas, feelings, desires, and perceptions—someone who will help us to grow through self-disclosure. This may be, for some of us, our spouses; for others, a good friend in the ministry; for others, a friend outside the vocation; and for others, a professional counselor. We may find, and I think it's a foregone conclusion, that even with all the risks, the benefits of self-disclosing are well worth it. We also may find ourselves incorporating the skills of self-disclosure into our professional relationships in the parish as well, and this can only enhance our ministry.

Of course, self-disclosure is not deemed appropriate for every situation, and we pastors need to be cognizant of that fact. Adler, Rosenfeld, and Towne (Interplay: The Process of Interpersonal Communication, 4th ed.) list seven guidelines for self-disclosing which might prove helpful to us. 1) Is the other person important to you? Is your relationship valued sufficiently enough to disclose significant parts of yourself? 2) Is the risk of disclosing reasonable? Are the probable benefits worth the possible adverse consequences? How likely are the imagined horrors of opening up to occur? 3) Is the self-disclosure appropriate? Is the existing relationship at a stage where self-disclosure can be mutually beneficial? Is this the right time for the other person to respond in a supportive manner, or is the other person in a time-crunch, preoccupied, in a bad mood, or overtired? 4) Is the disclosure relevant to the situation at hand? Recalling the Star of Introspection, is the self-disclosure directly related to the "here and now" as opposed to the "there and then?" 5) Is the disclosure reciprocated? If this is not a formal, therapeutic relationship, such as with your physician, is the other person willing to "balance" the relationship with some disclosure of her/his own? 6) Will the effect be constructive? Somewhat related to the first guideline, will your disclosures disable the other person at great cost to the relationship? Will it help more than it hurts? 7) Is the self-disclosure clear and understandable? Referring again to the Star of Introspection, are the perceptions being shared explicitly enough so as not to be overly vague and easily misunderstood?

Adler, et al, (Interplay, 4th ed.), close their chapter on Self-Disclosure with these words: "The amount and type of information we share with others defines the scope and quality of our relationships. What to reveal, who to honor with this personal information, and how to disclose are questions every communicator needs to ask." I can only say "Amen" to that.

On the subject of appropriateness, there's one more thing that needs mentioning, especially for anyone communicating in the public arena, pastors included. The appropriateness of public self-disclosure is always a judgment call, especially since it is so culturally-bound. When a televangelist recounts his sins over the television set, that might be acceptable according to some cultural standards, while for others it may not. One congregation might accept as appropriate the pastor's disclosing of her/ his family interaction as support for a sermonic point, while another congregation with a different ethnic or professional background may not. Disclosing elements of one's own spousal relationship may be rhetorically powerful in a sermon or to make a point in a church group, but it may not always be culturally appropriate. Disclosing how affectionate one feels toward another person's spouse, however platonic that feeling might be, may not be deemed acceptable or appropriate by the people of a particular parish because of recent events in the community or the dominant cultural teaching in that community of which recent events become a reinforcing part.

The skill of self-disclosing is important for every pastor to have. Acknowledging the risks, and they are especially frightening for a public figure, the benefits are too great not to have this skill in one's communication repertoire. If we as pastors hope to develop trusting relationships with our people, we need to become involved in appropriate and skillful self-disclosing.

Chapter Eight
Defensiveness

And the Lord sent Nathan to David. He came to him, and said to him, "There were two men in a certain city, the one rich and the other poor. The rich man had very many flocks and herds; but the poor man had nothing but one little ewe lamb, which he had bought. And he brought it up, and it grew up with him and with his children; it used to eat of his meager fare, and drink from his cup, and lie in his bosom, and it was like a daughter to him. Now there came a traveler to the rich man, and he was loath to take one of his own flock or herd to prepare for the wayfarer who had come to him, but he took the poor man's lamb, and prepared that for the guest who had come to him." Then David's anger was greatly kindled against the man. He said to Nathan, "As the Lord lives, the man who has done this deserves to die; he shall restore the lamb fourfold, because he did this thing, and because he had no pity." Nathan said to David, "You are the man!"

II Samuel 12:1-7a NRSV

If anyone had cause to be defensive, it was David. His whole image as a moral leader to his people was in jeopardy. He knew the truth had been uncovered and now lay naked before the eyes of this wily prophet of God. David could have tried to explain away his action, somehow to clothe it in moral garments; but he didn't. He could have told

Nathan to mind his own business, mount the attack against his accusor and thereby divert attention from himself; but he didn't. He could have employed any number of defensive maneuvers to protect himself against the accusations being made; but he didn't. What David did do was to admit the truth: "I have sinned against the Lord." This is but one illustration, from literally thousands available in Scripture, of situations and relationships in which defensive behavior was either evident or possible.

Just what is defensiveness? Adler and Towne, in Looking Out/Looking In, define it as "the attempt to protect a public image that we perceive is being attacked." This sounds like a simple, clearcut, easily identifiable definition and concept, but it is far more than that. Defensiveness does include public (or "presented") image, but also one's privately-held image of what one purposely hides from the public. The subject includes alternatives of action, such as availability and use of defense mechanisms and methods of responding to both positive and negative criticism. It includes at least a glance at the kind of communication climate which promotes defensiveness and the kind that mitigates against it. In this chapter, I will attempt to look at all these aspects of defensiveness, particularly as they apply to the work of the pastor in the parish, in hopes that a better understanding of the subject will remove this greatest barrier to interpersonal communication in the pastor's life (or anyone else's, for that matter).

As I stated in Chapter Two, human beings will do almost anything to perpetuate an existing self-concept. We'll lie to others; we'll construct complex fantasies to convince ourselves; we'll reorganize our perceptions; we'll attack, withdraw, or otherwise strategize our personal and public interaction; all attempts to defend the image of ourselves we want to present to others. As some communication analysts have termed it, we put on "masks" so others will see the person we want them to see, though we do not always do it successfully.

Whatever we *really* think of ourselves, however we *really* see ourselves, as pastors many of us have been enculturated to present to others, especially to the people of our parishes, a certain public image, a presented-self. Oftimes the denominations we serve set the basic parameters for the image we are "supposed" to project, and the behaviors which emanate from it. Those of us who do not "fit" that image naturally, that is, who do not have a similar private image of self, and who still want to work within the system, soon discover an increasing dissimilarity between our two self-images: our private one and our presented one. There are a number of ways we have learned to live with this situation, some more comfortably than others, from keeping our home life very private and separated from our vocational life, to finding kindred spirits in the ministry with whom "we can be ourselves," to the secret behavior involved in occasional geographic distancing. When we can separate these two selves successfully, as many of us do, only the presented-self occasionally will be threatened (our perception of threat, of course) and require defending. If we cannot separate our two self-images distinctly and acceptably, we will spend time, when we perceive ourselves challenged, justifying the relationship we have constructed between our private and public behavior (justification being one of the forms of defense). Our employed defense mechanisms become the interpersonal communication barrier called "defensiveness" when they are used *habitually* in the attempt, whether conscious or not, to protect this or any unrealistic image of self; that is, whenever our public image does not jibe with who we really know ourselves to be but are unwilling to admit. If I have accepted as legitimate and desirable the description of "a good pastor" as one who calls in every parish home at least once a year, and it is expected by the people in my congregation, but I do not do it because I am either uncomfortable or simply do not like to make calls, even when someone innocently asks how the visitation program is going, I may verbalize all kinds of reasons why I have not made the calls, whether those reasons are true or not. My privately-seen self is not a caller; my presented-self is supposed

174

to be a caller. I may need to construct reasons why I have not lived up to my presented-self responsibilities, the construction of which is called "rationalization," one of the many recognizable defense-mechanisms employed to defend an unreal image-of-self.

There would be no great problems with all this, for it often seems little more than game-playing, and most people seem to participate to one degree or another, if it were not for the longer range effects, one of which is the likelihood that the defensive behavior will lower the perceived trust level of the defensive person. When someone reacts defensively to something I communicate, I wonder what's behind their reaction, what they're not saying, what they're covering up. Suspecting that the other person is rationalizing, particularly in contrast to "obvious" fact, tends to make us suspicious, as does regression, or unwarranted aggression, or any of the other defense mechanisms. And, of course, as we all have experienced, and research bears this out, suspicion is detrimental to relationships, in that it questions how much honest self-disclosure is occurring and how open the other person really is.

A second long-range effect of habitual defensiveness is not getting to know the defensive person as a unique individual, as a person with characteristics, abilities, experiences, and perceptions that I can learn to appreciate and the knowledge from which I can further my own growth and understanding of life. When another person behaves defensively with me, I lose an opportunity for my own growth.

A more immediate, and potentially long-range, effect of defensive communication is its tendency to spiral in intensity. This "spiral effect," as communicologists have called it, is the reciprocal behavior that occurs when someone becomes defensive, and that defensive behavior elicits a self-protective response from the first person, whose defensiveness tends to evoke further defensive behavior from the second person, and on and on, until someone breaks the spiral, or the relationship is severely damaged. The speed and intensity of this spiral of "relationship disintegration," as I am prone to label it, will depend in great measure on the kinds of defense mechanisms that are employed; for example, verbal aggression will probably move disintegration along much faster and more intensely than will rationalization or regression. Whether it be immediate or longer range in its effect, the defensive spiral often occurs and almost always adversely affects the relationship.

I have mentioned the term "defense mechanisms" many times without describing precisely what they are. Now is the time to do so. There are a number of such mechanisms or reactive behaviors available to us, each designed to work with certain personalities and be applied to particular situations in which we find ourselves. These mechanisms, which most observors of the human scene can identify with minimum effort, are strategies for "mask-wearing," for the purpose of misrepresentation of self. It is particularly difficult for us in the clergy to admit such behavior, even when we do catch ourselves doing it. The standard for behavior which we impose upon ourselves and to which we hold ourselves accountable—the ideal, perfect self—is so very difficult to attain that it might be regarded as unrealistic. However unrealistic it may be, many of us seem to believe that it needs defending when challenged or we perceive ourselves being attacked. Thus, we in the clergy, along with the unrealisticly-high-status physician in our society, might use more defense-mechanisms than the average person, and more frequently. Being public people in the public eye, we are "fair game" for attack, and "need to be on guard" (ready to use whatever defense-mechanisms that are available and will work for us), lest our public-self be damaged or destroyed. The more we use these defense-mechanisms in protecting our presenting-self, the more we tend to convince ourselves that what we're trying to protect is, indeed, our real self. When we get caught up in this, our ministry takes on the appearance of being more reactive than pro-active, usually a very counterproductive situation.

Again, I appreciate and have found most helpful the writing of Adler and Towne in their <u>Looking</u>

<u>Out/Looking In</u>. They describe twelve of the more common defense mechanisms we use. (In later editions, they compressed these twelve into six and seven, but I prefer their earlier labeling.) The first is *rationalization*, thinking up a logical but untrue or misleading explanation of behavior, usually after the fact, designed to protect an unrealistic picture we have of ourselves. The aforementioned example on one's aversion to pastoral calling illustrates rationalization: "I do not have time to make calls with the hours I put in on my sermon preparation and then there's always an unexpected funeral or emergency at the church; besides, many people resent the intrusion nowadays." All these "reasons" may be partially true; however, the most basic reason is seldom mentioned because it may not be convincing to the questionner or supportive of the pastor's ideal (but unrealistic) self-image. The more a pastor rationalizes, the more convinced s/he becomes of its truth. And the more parishoners perceive these reasons as defensiveness, the less trust they will have in the pastor.

A second defense-mechanism is *compensation*. This is a frequently used technique to avoid dealing with a perceived personal shortcoming, when someone either directly or indirectly mentions it. The pastor who recognizes a limited ability to work with people in small groups in a democratic fashion, when s/he perceives someone focusing on this personal shortcoming, may divert attention to the pastor's recognized strength in moral and visionary leadership which necessitates individual decisionmaking. Instead of facing the shortcoming head on, admitting it and possibly doing something about it, the pastor will "compensate" by noting and/or spending more time on a recognizable strength. This is another form of defensiveness, too much of which can create frustration, mistrust, a weakening of relationships, and consequently missed opportunities for both growth and ministry.

Reaction formation refers to a defense mechanism which avoids the problem someone mentions, and which is perceived as a form of personal attack, and then dealt with by acting in an exaggerated opposite manner. I once knew a minister who viewed himself as inferior to his fellow clergy—they could articulate their theology and social concerns so much better than he could, so he thought—and in contrast to the way he felt, he became very domineering in his relationships with them, pontificating frequently, even to the point of being bombastic. He was employing reaction formation as his form of defensive behavior, acting in an exaggerated opposite manner from the way he really felt. Over the years his colleagues became very tired of this defensive behavior and increasingly avoided him, thus causing him to intensify both his feeling of inferiority and his unappreciated defensiveness.

Then there's the favorite of many, the defense

mechanism called *projection*. With this one we isolate an undesirable behavior or characteristic of our own, and project it onto another person or group of persons, the result being we don't have to handle it ourselves. Having lived through a number of church building programs, I have heard ad nauseum the comment: "That's going to bother some people," or "There's a lot of people who aren't going to like that," whether the issue be red carpeting in the sanctuary, or the color of sunshine in a church school room. Members of a building committee often express their own objections to something being proposed by projecting their objection onto someone "out there." The ugliest (my value judgment) example of projection I've ever encountered in an official church group was the time during the 1960's when our bishop requested each local church body to discuss and make a determination if that congregation would welcome a black pastor, should one be appointed to serve there. Many suburban churches really wrestled with this one! The discussion I witnessed included statements like: "I, personally, wouldn't mind, because I'm not prejudiced, but I know a number of people who wouldn't accept a black pastor here and would leave the church if one were appointed;" and "We've just entered a building program, and we can't take any chances not being able to meet our mortgage payments, so we can't afford to have a black minister here because people would leave and take their money with them." That church body sent a letter to the bishop requesting that a black minister not serve there, because he would not be welcome, too many "others" in the congregation would object. As I said, an ugly example of projection.

Projection might be employed by a pastor developing a case of "burnout." Instead of dealing directly with her/his own problem of diminishing enthusiasm, the pastor may spend time blaming the congregation for their lack of spiritual energy. Instead of working on activities which could rejuvenate her/his own spiritual life, such as increased time in study and/or meditation, or attending a retreat, or talking it over with some confidant, such a pastor will castigate the congregation in the sermon (sometimes not very subtly) for their lack of commitment, or develop the habit of complaining to anyone who will listen about the deadbeats in the congregation, and all s/he could do if they were a bit more enthusiastic about their church. Yes, projection is a handy defense mechanism which diverts the focus from the real root of the problem.

Identification is another usable defense mechanism for some people. Pastors use it by being overly involved in patterning their ministry after some well-known and successful clergyperson. Imitation may well be the highest compliment one can give, but putting too much energy into it results

181

in artificiality. Leo Buscaglia once said something like, "Be the best person you can be. Don't try to be another Leo Buscaglia, because I'm the best one there is, so you'll always be second best." Foster Wilcox should concentrate on being the best Foster Wilcox there is, and not spend the bulk of his energies avoiding this task by trying to be another Harry Emerson Fosdick. Were he to do the latter, his ministry would tend to lose its genuineness and become an act.

Not long ago, I visited a church whose members exerted considerable energy on being like the large, seemingly very successful church in a neighboring community. Instead of developing its own unique ministry using the multiple and enviable talents of its own membership, this church lived the life of a "copycat," not responding to its own situation in a genuine way, but rather second-handedly applying the other church's proven programs. It communicated artificiality. Here was a congregation with all kinds of possibility in ministry which had developed an unrealistic self-image and spent too much time defending it through identification, rather than working on its own unique situation. Much of the blame for its limited success could be laid at the feet of its pastoral leadership, who felt a greater need to identify than to minister.

The next defense mechanism to look at is called *fantasy.* This is more than the short daydream we all need occasionally to relieve the drudgery of some tiresome task. Fantasy here is escaping into a dream world of one's own in order to avoid applying oneself to the task of change or self-improvement. It is creating a more exciting, interesting, and satisfying existence through one's dreams, rather than working to better the real one. Sometimes I wonder if whole congregations and maybe even some entire denominations defend themselves against accusations of ineffectiveness by living in a dream world of their own, the fantasy of the church in a New Testament world, rather than working to apply the Gospel to the modern world in which they do live. I wonder how many pastors encourage this kind of fantasizing as a defense against the "slings and arrows" of contemporary cultures, rather than meeting their challenge in a proactive way. When some religious people endorse withdrawing from the modern world, I wonder if their desire is based more on a very human defensive posture than it is on anything they read in the Bible. Fantasizing, as a defense mechanism, is not limited to those who try to escape their own boring lives by watching the television soaps!

Next: *repression*, denying the existence of a problem, or "forgetting it away," simply putting it out of one's mind or consciousness as if it didn't really exist (which it doesn't in the mind of the person adept at repressing). Rather than facing up to an unpleasant situation, the repressor protects the self by not consciously recognizing either the unpleasantness or the entire situation, or both. Any pastor who has worked with families with alcohol or other drug problems has seen this defense mechanism used effectively to avoid dealing with the problem: simply deny its existence. "So and so may drink too much occasionally, and become abusive, but there's no real problem." "So and so may smoke pot once in awhile, don't all teenagers?, but s/he's been stoned only once that I know about; there's no problem."

The group personality of a congregation can also participate in repression. I heard about one local church that "went through pastors faster than the most hyped cathartic." No pastor stayed there more than eighteen months, most leaving within a year. However, no one ever admitted there was a problem (except when they involved themselves in a little projection and accused all ministers of being stubborn and cantankerous!). As long as there was no problem, they didn't have to deal with it!

Dependency or regression is the next defense mechanism to look at, when a person behaves like a child, mouthing "I can't" or a variation of it when confronted with a request or pressure to do something s/he doesn't like or want to do. Rather than admit the decision is a matter of the will, or a choice of options, or an application of priorities, the regressor will attempt to protect the self-image by saying, "Gee, I'd like to, but I can't." The minister might peer into her/his little black date book, sometimes luckily finding a previous appointment and sometimes only an empty space, never so the requestor can see the calendar, and, not wanting either to attend that meeting or to damage the self-image, say, "Oh, I'm sorry, I can't; something else is scheduled then. Maybe some other time." The pastor who is self-convinced that s/he just "can't" find time to spend with the children, is admitting a helplessness not unlike when s/he was a young child, rather than owning up to the fact that prioritizing has occurred, and the children are lower on the priority list than the church work. Wanting to believe oneself as a good parent, it's much easier to say, "I'm sorry; I *can't* be with you tonight at your track meet. I have to work on my sermon," rather than to say, "I'm sorry there's a conflict, but my sermon preparation has a higher priority right now than your track meet, so I won't be there." Besides, the pastor *could* do both by going to the track meet, then working on the sermon into the wee hours of the night. S/he is *choosing* not to do this. "I can't" substitutes for "I choose not to." Regression: a very convenient defense mechanism.

This behavior is convenient for a congregation, too. A local church "caught" in the expanding inner-city says, "We can't grow. We're hemmed in by people not interested in our church." A choice has been made not to adapt to the changing population and its needs, a matter of will, but the local church "defends" its image as a concerned people simply by complaining that it *can't* grow! Change takes energy, and such a church body, were it willing to put in the necessary time and effort, probably could grow; but often it chooses not to, yet is unwilling to admit that fact, not even to itself.

A defense mechanism a pastor occasionally encounters in counseling is called *emotional insulation*, or sometimes *apathy*. Rather than face some painful situation or unpleasant relationship, a person avoids hurt by simply not getting involved or pretending not to care. Often this is a person who has been hurt badly in the past and isn't going to put her/himself into that position again. Once the heart, having been "worn on the sleeve," gets banged around, a person is not likely to become so vulnerable again. It seems easier just to communicate "I don't care." The problem with that defensive posture is that it's just another strategy for avoiding the problem. As long as I communicate not caring, when I really do care, I won't work on the problem because that would admit caring.

It is indeed tragic when a pastor or a congregation exercises this defense mechanism. We are good and likable people, and when someone rejects our overtures, that rejection doesn't fit our self-image, and we are sometimes tempted to react to that rejection with a "we don't care." The trouble with this apathetic response is that it invites the rejector not to care as well (the spiral effect, again).

This is definitely not the message our churches or pastors should be communicating, if we are serious about our mission! Our relationship with others has little chance of growing if we will not admit to caring for those whom we serve, caring to the point of being willing to be hurt.

Displacement is another convenient and tempting defense mechanism to employ. This is the venting of aggressive or hostile feelings against objects or persons perceived as less dangerous than the person or persons who provoked the feelings originally. One time when I was experiencing a particularly stressful time with the Administrative Board of the local church I served, I decided to build a deck on our lake cabin. Each nail in that large deck became a board member to be hammered symbolically. I was displacing my anger and frustration onto an inanimate object that couldn't argue. This was relatively harmless, only a bruised thumb, occasionally; however, it did nothing to alleviate the tension of board meetings. Rather than risk the greater pain of confrontation, I "took it out on" my deck nails. If I had displaced my anger and frustration onto my dog by kicking her, that would have been cruel and inhumane. Worse yet, I could have displaced onto my children, expressing my hostility toward board members by screaming at or slapping those who were less powerful than I and who probably wouldn't retaliate. Child abuse is frequently the expression of defensiveness through displacement. I wonder, occasionally, if acts of vandalism in our communities and churches are sometimes expressions of displacement as well.

Undoing is another interesting defense mechanism that is sometimes used to protect one's own self-image. This is the act of making up for something done or said that is regretted. Though it may seem to be a symbolic gesture of apology, it is really a defense mechanism when its purpose is to signal to the person that's hurt, "See, I'm not really such a bad guy after all." Parents who feel guilty after administering discipline to their children sometimes employ undoing as a defensive measure to support their self-image as "good" parents worthy of their children's affection. After a spanking or a grounding, a parent might suggest an ice cream cone later, of course after sufficient time to allow the discipline to be understood. Many a time a plate of cookies has found its way to the parsonage after a confrontation between a layperson and the pastor over some church policy or matter. The ice cream and the cookies can be considered undoing if those acts are only attempts to reinforce the ideal self-image of always being a "nice person." If they are sincere expressions of apology or signals of an actual change in behavior, that is something else. However, if undoing happens frequently, one begins to wonder.

The last of the twelve defense mechanisms Adler and Towne describe is *verbal aggression.* This is the counterattacking maneuver of diverting attention away from the threatened self-image by drawing attention to the other person's faults or by throwing a temper tantrum or by sarcasm or in some way embarrassing the perceived attacker. I have "heard tell" of ministers who have administered verbal aggression and abuse from the pulpit, more often than not in the form of cutting remarks and sarcasm, when they have felt their image as a faithful pastor was threatened by some members of the congregation. I once chatted with a young minister so threatened who laughingly admitted that when he was criticized by members of his congregation, he just preached more loudly about *their* sin, of course never mentioning names, but they knew whom he was talking about. I don't know if this was fact or fantasy on his part; I do know that it serves as an excellent example of using the defensive power of verbal aggression. Such a mechanism, like the other eleven, is subject to all the problems defensiveness creates.

Because we pastors are often perceived by members of our congregations as being more articulate than most people, that is able to use language to our advantage, few constituents dare to "take us on" and use verbal aggression with us as their defense-mechanism of choice when they feel we are threatening their self-image. Displacement, apathy, repression, fantasy, projection, and rationalization are the defense-mechanisms we are more likely to encounter when we purposely or inadvertantly threaten their self-images. It would be my guess, and I have no hard data to support this, that the defense mechanism chosen most frequently by members of our congregations when we regularly threaten their self-images is emotional insulation (apathy): "It doesn't matter." These people will look for another church to attend, or, worse yet, drop out until a new pastor arrives sometime in the future.

Jack Gibb has devoted much of his scholarly life to the study of defensiveness. In 1961 he wrote an article that is still referred to by most writers in the field of communication (Journal of Communication, Vol.11, No. 3). Besides identifying "the spiral effect," Gibb discovered six behaviors that tend to create a climate in which defensiveness is likely to occur. He then identified six contrasting behaviors that tended to do just the opposite, to create a climate in which the chance of defensiveness is reduced. He labeled the first list, "Defensive Behaviors," and the second list, "Supportive Behaviors." I much prefer calling the first list, "Defense-increasing Behaviors," and the second list, "Defense-reducing Behaviors," because it seems clearer to me and indicates that I can influence the existence and degree of defensive behavior in my relationships. Not only can I choose not to employ defense mechanisms in my own behavior, but I can also create a climate in which the other person will be less likely to become defensive. If I communicate with someone in any of the first six ways, that person will probably become somewhat defensive with me; if I communicate in any of the contrasting six ways, s/he will be less likely to act defensively. Since defensiveness is a major barrier to effective communication, I can influence to a large degree whatever success we achieve.

The Gibb Categories of Defensive and Supportive Behaviors

Defensive Behaviors............. *Supportive Behaviors*

1. Evaluation.................................... *1. Description*
2. Control .... *2. Problem Orientation*
3. Strategy .... *3. Spontaneity*
4. Neutrality .... *4. Empathy*
5. Superiority .... *5. Equality*
6. Certainty .... *6. Provisionalism*

When the other person perceives I am evaluating her/him, whether or not it's true matters little, s/he will tend to become defensive, ready to defend the self from an anticipated attack. One of my services to my denominational body has been to videotape the service of worship for any pastor or congregation who requests it, giving feedback to the pastor and the pastor-parish committee as we watch the playback together, concentrating on what the church might be communicating to any visitors and/or prospective members. Of course, this includes the sermon as well. Some pastors strongly resist this, even while admitting that they and their church might very well benefit from such an activity. One pastor, also a friend, whose lay committee requested my service, commented to me very sarcastically one time when I met him at a meeting: "I suppose you're coming to tell me how to preach!" He perceived evaluation (which wasn't true since all I do is to comment on what I perceive as the preacher's strengths) and became very defensive (verbal aggression, in this instance). After I described what I would be doing, describing his behavior in the chancel and the pulpit with the help of videotape, and that there would be no evaluation, either for him or for his committee or for the bishop, he softened and calmed down a bit, lessening his own defensiveness. When I moved, in his perception, from evaluating to describing, assuring him that he had no need to defend his self-image as an experienced preacher, we were much more at ease with each other and both looked forward to my time at his church.

Once in awhile a pastor will encounter someone in the congregation with a well developed need to control others. If such a person would strongly imply, for example, during a building campaign, that doing something her/his way might mean a larger contribution would be forthcoming, the pastor and some others in the congregation might well become a bit defensive. An attempt is being made to control their behavior and make them do something they wouldn't ordinarily do if the money weren't being held over their heads. On the other hand, if that person were to suggest her/his desire as one possible solution to the problem, the committee would be less likely to become defensive. They might even go along with it, knowing the suggestor would probably contribute more if they fell short. Moving from an attempt to control the behavior of others to a focus on the problem at hand reduces the tendency to act defensively. There is no longer a need to defend oneself because there is no perceived threat to the self-image. Everyone's focusing on the problem rather than attempting to control other people. However, every pastor should recognize, especially in a new parish where impressions are still being formed, that being problem-oriented may not be immediately accepted. Experience with persuasive sales techniques has taught most of us to be somewhat wary of motivation: "Is this some kind of trick? What's in it for him? Is he trying to control me?" Until problem-orientation is established as the modus operandi of the new pastor, such suspicions will exist. Only consistency and good humor will prevent the defensive spiral from taking over the relationship, driving in the wedges of mistrust and hostility.

Occasionally pastors inadvertantly create a defensive climate when the time of year rolls around to recruit parish leaders and committees. We strategize how to get positive responses by hedging a bit on the time required to do the job adequately; we fail to mention a disrupting problem they'll need to handle; we exaggerate their abilities to do the job; we might even conspire with a spouse or some other friend to encourage a "yes" to the nomination. We try to manipulate them into doing this important task for the church. If they are naive or innocent enough, they may never suspect the manipulation, do a good job, and no one is hurt. However, if they ever suspect they have been manipulated, tricked, or "used," a defensive climate will have been created with all its feelings of mistrust and self-protection.

On the other hand, spontaneity "puts the cards on the table," expresses feelings and thoughts of the moment, describes needs as perceived, allows the other to be a responsible human being, all adding up to honesty. Of course, both spontaneity and honesty need to be expressed with diplomacy and sensitivity, not to be confused with deviousness. Spontaneity may not get the slots on the nomination sheet all filled in, but it will create a more productive communication climate in the long run, and it does put the responsibility where it belongs.

Neutrality is another word for indifference. "It's OK. It doesn't matter," is an expression that can create a climate of defensiveness, especially if what is being responded to really *does* matter to the person saying it. Expressing lack of concern for something that deeply concerns another is a way of inviting frustration and anger, because it seems to imply an attitude, however temporary or permanent, that the other person's feelings are not very important—and that often translates into an attack on the worthwhileness of the person, creating a need for defense. Most of us pastors know this feeling intimately, especially when we encounter someone who is indifferent to us and to the work and mission of the church. That person touches a sensitive nerve, and it is not unusual for us to defend our existence. On the other hand, even when we meet someone strongly opposed to organized religion, we tend not to become so defensive simply because there is some empathy, some feeling, on the subject. Here is someone who cares, even if not agreeing.

In the counseling relationship, the person seeking help can often quickly sense whether or not the counselor really cares, or if s/he is indifferent, feigning concern. Perceived indifference will lead to a defensive response, and precious time will then need to be spent overcoming that barrier, and that person may not be willing to take the necessary time to do so, and an opportunity for ministering is lost. It takes considerable energy to communicate empathy, but it is essential in any pastoral relationship.

When someone acts superior, thrusting you into the inferior category, your response will most likely be one of defensiveness, probably seeking some way to "bring them down off their high horse." I remember one incident, of which I am not particularly proud, in which I reacted defensively to a perceived announcement of superiority. I had just moved into a new parish, in fact we were still unpacking, when the doorbell rang, and standing outside was an older man who identified himself as the other Protestant minister in this small town. In our conversation, he shared with me "who was who" in town as well as what was expected of a minister there. I remember one particular phrase which "stuck in my craw" during the entire time our ministries overlapped in that community: "I come to you as a Paul comes to a Timothy." With two successful pastorates behind me, I wasn't ready to accept that inferior role in this community, especially when the announcement was accompanied with a very paternalistic-sounding voice and a smothering arm across my shoulders. From that moment on, because of the communication climate of defensiveness which he tended to create, probably unconsciously, I had a very difficult time either trusting or liking that man.

If, in that initial conversation, he had said something less superior-sounding, things might have been different. "Welcome to our fair town. I look forward to wrestling with some new ideas. I've been here for five years now, and I've learned some things through trial and error. With your fresh insights and my experience here, maybe together we can make a difference." A welcome like this would have emphasized equality between us, and I would have been much more ready and willing to seek his advice. As it was, I generally avoided him wherever possible. Both of us were the poorer for it, and possibly our congregations, as well.

Gibb's final categories are certainty and provisionalism. Granted, there are many people who seem drawn to preachers who exude certainty in every dogmatic statement they utter. There does seem to be a desire for absolute certainty in many parts of our society today. However, there are just as many of us, maybe more, who do not react so positively to certainty (as Gibb defines it), but who are rather "turned off" by such expression. Certainty here is the communicated attitude that one's way of looking at something or someone, or one's way of doing something is the *only* way that's right or proper. We pastors, because of the nature of our faith and work, are often perceived by others as certain. We should be aware that this communicated attitude results in at least a degree of resistance. When we send the message that we are not open to any additional insights, that there are no other existent facts which are available or worth considering, we encourage an atmosphere which spawns defensive feelings. In summary, on this particular question or issue, we know it all. And that tends to turn people off, except those, of course, who seem to have a deep psychological need to be led.

In Gibb's other list, we find the word "provisionalism," a label which does not mean "being wishy-washy," though some absolute dogmatists often perceive it as such. This defense-reducing communication behavior *does* allow for position-taking, although not with a dogmatist's certainty. The provisionalist is one who forms a belief-system or takes a position using all the facts, information, situation, relationships, etc. available at the moment. This person is one who is open to new information which might alter her/his perception. Such a person communicates an attitude of openness to and appreciation for the insights of other people, insights which even might cause some idea-adjustment and self-behavioral changes. The provisionalist is *sure*, but never *so* sure that all new information, insights, or possibilities are automatically excluded from consideration and evaluation. Communicating this provisionalist's attitude, even in the preaching function, but especially in interpersonal relationships, reduces the listeners' need to protect a self-image. Showing interest in that which is not yet known to you encourages participation and communication in others; whereas certainty often only challenges the other person to find the flaw in your argument, one of the many forms of defensive behavior.

Obviously, these attitudes are not expressed in isolation from each other. They are often communicated in combination; for example, someone who communicates provisionally also tends to express problem orientation and equality. The person who seems certain also tends to be a controller who acts superior. The problem oriented person also tends to be descriptive and more spontaneous; whereas the controller will often strategize and be judgmental. The goal of the person who would be a more effective communicator is to communicate more with the six defense-reducing behaviors and less with the six defense-raising behaviors. I am convinced that the pastor who does this will have a happier and more productive ministry. I should mention here that the spiral effect we've already discussed occurs just as readily with defense-reducing behaviors as it does with defense-raising behaviors. Once the initial, culturally-taught suspicion is overcome, given sincerely religious people, reciprocal behaviors will be forthcoming. Creating this kind of positive climate for communication is bound to produce a more trusting environment in which spiritual growth can result, both for the pastor and for the congregation.

Possibly one of the most difficult communication

situations which a pastor encounters is in receiving and responding to the inevitable criticism that comes. Leaders in every organization should expect to be criticized; however, many pastors seem to think they get more than their share. This may or may not be true. A case may be built either way. Be that as it may, the wise pastoral communicator will practice the kind of response to criticism that will not result in escalating the spiral of defensiveness.

Unfortunately, most criticism is not given and received within a positive communication climate. Even though the words are heard, "This is meant to be *constructive* criticism," it frequently is not perceived that way. Animosity is often present. The need to control or to feel superior is sometimes fairly obvious. These perceptions add up to a rather negative communication climate. In this kind of environment, how does a pastor respond to criticism?

At least eight distinct choices are available to a person who wants to respond to criticism offered in a negative communication environment and, at the same time, attempt to transform the negative climate into a more positive one. This may sound like an impossible task, but it is not. For my example of criticism-responding, I will use a common complaint of some parishioners in a few of our "mainline" Protestant churches: "Your preaching is not Biblical enough. You should

200

preach the Bible more—as it is written!"

The first method of responding to criticism given in a negative climate is to seek more information. This can be done in two ways: *ask* for specifics and *guess* about specifics. Asking for specifics after the abovementioned criticism might be worded this way: "I don't understand exactly what you mean. I thought I was applying the Bible's teaching to our world today. Can you give me some examples where my preaching is not Biblically-based?—where I need to change?" Guessing about specifics might sound this way: "Are you referring to this morning's sermon? Or are you objecting to the one I preached last month on the philosophy of military deterrance?" In both of these cases, the pastor is seeking more information, both to understand the criticism and to learn from it. Whether or not the criticism is valid, the pastor is communicating a willingness to listen and the worthwhileness of the person criticizing, thus turning a potentially destructive exchange into one with the possibility of mutual growth.

A second way to respond to criticism given in a negative environment is to reflect back the criticizer's ideas, and in doing so communicate a desire to understand the criticism, using the listening skills discussed in Chapter Six. "Am I understanding you correctly that you think my preaching is not based on a Scriptural foundation and that I should only preach on subjects actually discussed in the Bible?" The advantage to this is accuracy; in just a few moments a pastor can find out what the core of the criticism is. Sometimes understanding of the perception or acknowledgment of the issue is all the criticizer really wants. Hearing the problem verbalized may satisfy the critical feeling, put it into perspective, and neutralize intense and potentially harmful relational feelings.

A third way to respond to criticism is to ask about the consequences of your behavior. "What harmful effects do you think my style of preaching has caused? What do you think will happen to this congregation if I continue to preach as I have?" Looking at the criticizer's perceptions may be an important learning experience for a pastor, giving insight into something not heretofore understood. On the other hand, in asking about possible consequences, a pastor might realize how effective s/he has really been, and what is being expressed is a fear of an overly-comfortable faith being challenged. In either case, a criticism has been heard, the worth of the criticizer has been acknowledged, and a potential disruption to a pastoral relationship has been averted.

A fourth way to respond to criticism in a negative climate is to solicit additional complaints. "Is there anything more about my pastoral work here that bothers you?" This may seem rather ridiculous, but only on the surface. Seldom will a pastoral critic have a ready list of gripes, and getting the critic to see this particular criticism in perspective often dulls its excessive importance at the moment. If, indeed, there are other complaints, this is an effective way of learning what they are; or, this criticism might even be a smokescreen for something else the criticizer wants to suggest that the pastor work on. If the latter is the case, the critic will be satisfied that the pastor is willing to listen and even to work on making the ministry more effective, and, who knows, the pastor may have found an ally (or, in the least, some loyal opposition).

The last four choices of response to criticism are variations of agreement. However, agreement is not necessarily the passive acceptance of criticism that communicates the losing side of a win/lose situation. Even if the pastor honestly cannot agree with the criticism per se, there is almost always something in the critical content or intent or relationship with which the pastor can agree. The first kind of agreement is agreeing with whatever truth is indisputable, the choice of response David made to Nathan. "You're right, my preaching is not Biblical enough for some people. I know there are some within the congregation who think I should preach more directly from the Bible." If the statement is true, why should the pastor not admit it openly? Why become defensive and drive a wedge between oneself and the critic, unless the pastor really is trying to defend an unrealistic self-image, in which case there might be more here than a communication problem? Of course, it is not only what is said in the criticism that bothers us, usually it is the perceived evaluation that accompanies it that we most resist. Once the pastor learns to accept the content of a criticism, and separate it from any accompanying perceived evaluation, s/he will be exercising a response that is both honest and nondefensive. Frequently a critic only wants an argument, one that must be settled in a win/lose fashion, and agreeing with the obvious truth blunts that goal and at the same time keeps open the possibliity for further discussion.

The second kind of agreement one can make to a critic is agreeing with the odds. "It's possible my approach is as influencial as you fear and its flattering to imagine that, but chances are people only hear what they want to hear anyway, Biblical passages or not." Here the preacher is acknowledging the criticism as well as the possibility of the implied consequences, even though not acquiescing to them. If the criticism is genuine and is being made without a hidden agenda, possible though unlikely in a negative communication climate, the critic knows it has been heard and the pastor is not discounting its validity— agreeing with the odds, even though not submitting to the behavioral change. The relationship, for whatever its worth, is still intact; the defensive spiral has not built an insurmountable barrier.

A third kind of agreement with a critic in a negative communication climate is agreeing in principle. "I agree, I would like my preaching to be more Biblical, but I'm not sure the congregation would listen very long without contemporary application and cultural interpretation." With a response such as this, the pastor is agreeing with the principle of Biblical preaching, and is indicating a desire to take the criticism seriously, at the same time communicating that the decision to do otherwise is based on something other than an "anti-Biblical" attitude. Admitting to a basic agreement (the principle) with the critic also invites a less defensive discussion on the subject, one that probably would bring to light differing interpretations of Scripture and approaches to its application, and in a way that might improve the relationship.

As difficult as it is to respond to a critic with some form of agreement, the results of such behavior are often well worth the effort. Our natural inclination is to jump to our own defense with some mechanism that will adequately protect our self-image, rather than listen to the criticism, take from it what is helpful, overlook or ignore any perceived judgment, and not allow the criticism to adversely affect our relationship. It is unrealistic to suggest that it is *always* possible to find some aspect of a criticism with which one can agree. Once in awhile the criticism is so far off the mark that no degree of agreement is possible. However, most of us probably would be very surprised how often we can agree with a criticism, or at least some part of it.

Some of our critics will not be satisfied with only verbal agreement, but will expect us to change our behavior. Agreeing with a critic is an effective nondefensive response, until the critic asks what we plan to do about it. When this occurs, we have moved into the subject of "conflict management," the subject of the next chapter.

Before I discuss the troublesome topic of managing conflict, I should like to say something about responding to criticism when it is given in a positive communication climate, when the environment is devoid of defensive feelings, or at least they are manageably at a minimum. How is this positive climate sustained once it is achieved?

Besides being mindful of Jack Gibb's list of six supportive behaviors discussed earlier, there are a few other behaviors worth remembering, too, some of which are implied above, but are important enough to discuss briefly here. First, when receiving criticism, acknowledge the other person. Though this may sound simple, it is sometimes overlooked or just taken for granted. One way of acknowledging is to employ the positive listening skills discussed in Chapter Six, particularly active or reflective (my adjective was "relational") listening in an effort to understand the critic and the criticism, that is, both the content of the criticism and the feelings of the critic. Both are important, sometimes one more than the other. It is wise to sort out which is the main thrust of the encounter, to understand it, and to deal with that first. In other words, acknowledging the other person is to take that person seriously, whether or not the criticism is perceived as valid.

Secondly, to sustain a positive communication climate in the presence of a personal criticism, the pastor should demonstrate an open-minded attitude. A reaction of immediate argument is not demonstrating such an attitude. An invitation to work out differences, or at least to find a way to be more comfortable with differences, is. Presenting a closed mind invites defensiveness and strains relationships.

Thirdly, agree whenever possible. Even though some lasting relationships have a large number of disagreements, the relationship is based primarily on agreement, even if it is an agreement to disagree. In agreeing, in discovering some common principles and perspectives, in acknowledging points of agreement, individuals mesh into relational units. To keep a conversational relationship intact, whether it be momentary or long term, agreement on something is necessary, and the more that is discovered (or uncovered) on which there is agreement, the more positive the communication climate will be.

Fourth, to sustain this positive climate in the face of personal criticism, the pastor should show concern and appreciation for the other person's interests. If the critic didn't care at all, about the subject, the situation, or the relationship, probably no criticism would have been offered in the first place. The opposite of concern, as it is with love, is not antagonism or hate, but indifference. A critic cares. A critic is interested, especially one who is communicting in an already established positive climate. A pastor's open acknowledgment of the critic's interest and concern can only have a positive effect on the relationship.

Lastly, the pastor should communicate honestly. Sounding almost like an unnecessary cliche, it is more taken for granted than it is actual. Honesty here is more than exchanging ideas; it includes the sharing of real feelings. It is diplomatically saying what is on one's mind and in one's heart. It is not structuring "little white lies" to save someone's feelings (usually one's own), lies which must be remembered and covered up with more lies. Few things cloud a communication climate more than being caught in a lie, even a "small" one, if there is such a thing. An honest response to a criticism, accompanied by acknowledgment of the other person, an open-minded attitude, an attempt to agree whenever possible, and showing concern for the other person's interest, will almost guarantee the continuance of the positive communication climate in which a personal criticism is made.

It isn't easy to drop one's defensive posture, be it in international relations or in interpersonal relationships. It certainly wasn't easy for David to drop his defensiveness; however, to maintain the relationship with the Lord and with the prophet, Nathan, and to get on with life and the tasks at hand, taking the risk was the most effective way of handling the situation. If pastors wish to improve their communication skills, there is no more effective beginning place than putting effort into reducing their own defensive responses to criticism and creating a communication climate which will reduce the defensive behavior of their parishioners.

Chapter Nine
Conflict Management

Give ear to my prayer, O God; do not hide yourself from my supplication. Attend to me, and answer me; I am troubled in my complaint. I am distraught by the noise of the enemy, because of the clamor of the wicked. For they bring trouble upon me, and in anger they cherish enmity against me. . . And I say, "O that I had wings like a dove! I would fly away and be at rest; truly, I would flee far away; I would lodge in the wilderness; I would hurry to find a shelter for myself from the raging wind and tempest." Confuse, O Lord, confound their speech; for I see violence and strife in the city. . . It is not enemies who taunt me—I could bear that; it is not adversaries who deal insolently with me—I could hide from them. But it is you, my equal, my companion, my familiar friend, with whom I kept pleasant company; we walked in the house of God with the throng. . . My companion laid hands on a friend and violated a covenant with me with speech smoother than butter, but with a heart set on war; with words that were softer than oil, but in fact were drawn swords. Cast your burden on the Lord, and he will sustain you; he will never permit the righteous to me moved.

Psalm 55:1-3,6-9,12-14,20-22 NRSV

According to Edwin Poteat in The Interpreter's Bible, this Psalm is a poetic expression of David's conflict with Saul. I have chosen it out of the many examples of conflict in the Scriptures because David, in lamenting the distressed relationship,

211

considers alternative ways he could manage the conflict. He could run away ("I would fly away and be at rest"), or he could use force, albeit indirectly ("Confuse, O Lord, confound their speech"), or he could attempt to put the problem into a different perspective, what I shall later call "reframing," and ask the Lord for insight into the problem-conflict ("Cast your burden on the Lord"). David, in his poetic manner, is wrestling with his options in handling the conflict he perceives with his oppressor, probably Saul in this case.

Here, and throughout this chapter, I will not be using the expressions "resolving conflict" and "managing conflict" interchangably, for I believe to do so would be unfounded and misleading. All conflicts must, in some way, be managed; however, not all conflicts will be resolved. When a conflict *does* result in a satisfactory resolution, celebration is in order, for it does not happen as frequently as we would hope. On the other hand, I suppose, a conflict could be resolved in a way that would leave the parties unsatisfied, and such a result must be disappointing to all involved. Whatever the satisfaction level of a resolved conflict, the resolution itself is the result of the conflict being managed in a particular manner. Conflict resolution, therefore, is but the sometime outcome of conflict management.

Few, if any, people have experienced life without conflict. It seems to be an integral part of life today, or of any day, for that matter. I remember being told in a theatre class that drama would cease to exist without conflict, and in a psychology class that growth is impossible without conflict. It seems that conflict is part of the human condition, that it is a natural phenomenon. Therefore, the better part of wisdom is to learn how to manage it, rather than bemoan its existence. Such is the goal of this chapter.

There are three classic reasons given for the existence of conflict in human interaction. The first is "scarce resources." Where there is a perceived limit to the availability of resources necessary for human or cultural survival, or for the maintenance of a desired standard or mode of living, conflict for those resources will occur. On a worldwide scale, burgeoning populations need more land on which to grow their food or graze their animals, and since land is a limited resource, conflict often results as groups of people struggle for control and use of that land. On the local church level, conflict can result from multiple programs demanding access to a limited budget. A pastor encounters conflict when many people and opportunities for ministry make demands on the pastor's available time. There is only so much time (a scarce resource) in a day, in a week, and more and more people making demands upon it, that conflict is bound to occur, both among the parishioners as they perceive needs from their perspectives and within the pastor who is forced to prioritize the demands.

The second classic reason given for conflict is the presence of differing goals, and, of course, differing methods to achieve similar goals. Some people argue the relative merits of communism and capitalism as if each had a different goal, enslavement and freedom. Others argue that they have the same goal, the betterment of human life and society, but identify the conflict as different methods to reach that goal. The level of cooperation will depend upon the perception of the goals and the form of the argument, but both approaches will still result in some degree of conflict. In the local church, some people may want to build a large congregation and prestigious church, while others may want to keep the "family feeling" they knew when a child or when the church was small. Differing goals create conflict. Both groups may have a goal of meeting the spiritual needs of the community, but differ on how to accomplish the task, one believing it best to organize Bible study groups and invite people to them, and the other believing the best way would be to start a pre-school program in the church basement. Goals create an opportunity for conflict.

The third of the classic reasons for the presence of conflict in human society is the perception of relative power or powerlessness; that is, the amount of control a person (or a group of people) believes s/he has over her/his own life and destiny, in relation to another person (or group). This is the classic reason most frequently suggested in ethnic, racial, and gender conflict. It is argued that women, out of their long years of feeling powerless, are now bringing to surface a repressed conflict, based on their perceived lack of power in contrast to men's powerbase. Likewise it is argued that blacks are now demanding their own powerbase to counter the long-established white powerbase. Local churches with denominational affiliation sometimes conflict with the denomination's regulations and procedures, and are forced to manage the tension which emerges from the perception of relative power. Occasionally, this reason for conflict is at the root of lay/clergy tension in a parish, both in a traditionally authoritarian church or denomination (where the laypeople more often feel the conflict), and in a traditionally democratic church or denomination (where the clergy more often feel the conflict). Both are conflict situations because of the presence of perceived power and its relative distribution.

We humans do not seem to lack for communication-weapons to use in our conflict situations! We have a ready arsenal of strategies with which to fight our battles, and we pick and choose the best one for each conflict situation in which we find ourselves. Of course, each of us has a favorite weapon, one we rely on more frequently than others, and become so expert in its use that, eventually, it is seen as an extension of our personalities. What I am calling "weapons," Adler and Towne term "crazymakers," since their purpose is to drive others "crazy." They, in turn, are building on the work of George Bach, a leading authority on conflict and communication, who calls my "weapons" and Adler and Towne's "crazymakers" by another name: "strategies for dirty fighting," arguing that fighting per se is natural in a relationship and that it is only destructive when the fighting is dirty rather than clean or fair. Because such weapons are so recognizable for their frequent use, I will briefly describe a number of them so the pastor-reader can identify her/his own favorites and more dispassionately (not in the context of an actual conflict) evaluate their productivity in contrast to alternative modes of managing conflict.

Avoiding might well be the most used weapon of dirty fighting. The avoider simply refuses to fight by leaving, or pretending to be busy, or staring at the television, or some other way to ignore the conflict. Because this behavior is so frustrating, it creates even more tension and drives the other person crazy, and sustained long enough can mortally wound the relationship. The pastor who, because of a busy schedule, will not find a time to meet with the pastor-parish committee to discuss a growing rift in the congregation is dirty fighting with the weapon of avoidance.

Subject changing is another weapon in the arsenal of dirty fighting; it is a brand of avoiding. The subject changer fights by moving the conversation off subjects of potential conflict onto safer grounds. The problem/conflict is never addressed because whenever it is mentioned, the conversation suddenly is shifted to another topic, one that is "safer," at least for awhile; that is, until the other person gets so fed up that the relationship is severely damaged. Some pastors seem "theologically oriented" in all conversation, when, in reality, that may only be a ploy to move the subject away from the more sensitive and potentially volatile practical decision that must be made.

Gunnysacking is a favorite weapon of many people. It, too, is a version of avoiding, the kind that is temporary only. The gunnysacker puts each new little conflict, irritation, or problem into a gunnysack, not responding immediately but letting them pile up until the sack is bursting with all the accumulated frustration, and then when the object of the anger is least expecting it, dumps it all out before the unsuspecting and overwhelmed victim. Dirty fighting indeed! Pastors have been known to dump their gunnysacks from the pulpit onto unsuspecting congregations, a most inappropriate use of the preaching function, but very tempting— and dirty.

Pseudoaccommodating is another tempting

weapon to use. It, too, is a form of avoidance. The pseudoaccommodator is a game-player, a pretender who attempts to communicate that there's really nothing wrong, that no conflict exists, even if the other person adamantly insists there is. This difference, one who knows there is a problem-conflict and the other pretending that nothing is wrong, causes increasing tension and frequently a feeling of guilt and resentment toward the pseudoaccommodator. It's a weapon of dirty fighting that often backfires. Pastors are not beyond pretending occasionally, pretending that nothing's wrong, pretending that the church secretary is not really betraying confidences, in hopes that it will just go away. Sometimes we even justify such pretense with cliches like "Better not stir up a hornet's nest."

The last of the variations on avoiding is *joking*, kidding around when the other person wants to be serious, blocking the expression of important feelings when an issue is raised. Not wanting to face a conflict squarely out of fear or for whatever reason, the joker diverts attention with a funny story, a pun, a humorous jibe, or a clever but gentle putdown. This may be effective and welcome from time to time, but not as a constant diet. It becomes tiresome and resented after awhile. Pastors who joke around during times of conflict may find themselves not being taken seriously in other situations as well. Then, too, parishioners have been known to invite humor from the pastor to circumvent discussing a conflict that needs addressing; in other words, they get the pastor to wield the weapon of dirty fighting, and the problem is eliminated—until it emerges again in another form or situation.

Next on the weapon-rack is *distracting*, focusing attention on some unrelated "fault" of the other person in an attempt to elude a topic which could prove painful to oneself or the relationship. The new pastor who hasn't yet established a satisfactory working relationship with the "carryover" secretary or office manager, instead of facing squarely the upcoming conflict on managerial style and office procedures, may subtly (or not so subtly) question the secretary's ability to balance home responsibilities with the demands of the church office. Since this is rather paternalistic (or maternalistic),and somewhat demeaning, besides having nothing to do with the job itself, this may well be an attempt to circumvent the real conflict by using distraction as a weapon. Dirty fighting.

Next is *crisis tickling*, a weapon also known as hinting. A crisis tickler doesn't quite bring the conflict to the surface, content only to hint at what is wrong, expecting the other person to "bring up" the problem, thereby putting the onus for the problem onto the other. Unless that other person catches on that a conflict exists, it isn't pursued any further; however, the hinter cannot be blamed for an unattended conflict, since s/he did bring it up in the first place. Again, not a fair fighting technique, and certainly not a productive conflict management skill. A pastor who is concerned for racial or economic justice, and who only "dances around" the subject hinting that there are people "out there" who might have a problem with relating to minorities or the homeless, is guilty of approaching a conflict while waving the weapon of crisis tickling.

Guilt-making has sometimes been called, unfairly, "mother's weapon." It is the attempt to blame the other person for causing the guiltmaker unnecessary pain or anguish, trying to "get one's way" in a difference of opinion by a big sigh and the "martyr" look. Sometimes a pastor will use this weapon on the congregation, communicating a deep feeling of disappointment in their behavior in contrast to the pastor's own obvious struggle. Rather than risk an open confrontation on the issue at hand, a guiltmaking pastor is tempted to communicate instead "Poor me; look how you've let me down."

Mind reading is another technique from a dirty-fighter's weapon-rack. Instead of allowing the other person to be an equal adult with all rights and privileges of self-expression, the mind reader acts as an unsolicited analyst, suggesting reasons and motivations that may or may not exist in the other person's mind. This weapon is often identified by phrases like "I know what you're thinking" or "What you really mean is," and is used as a technique to divert attention from the issue to the other person's alleged inability to express an idea clearly or honestly. Instead of listening patiently to the relational problems a parishioner might be having with the pastor, the clergyperson might perceive a personal attack and decide to wield the weapon of mind reading as a short-cut to a solution and as an attempt to circumvent the basic issue. To do so is dirty-fighting.

Contract-tyrannizing is a very convenient weapon to be used by or on any employee, including the pastor of a church. Regardless of changing times and circumstances, the contract-tyrannizer will not alter behavior beyond what was originally agreed upon, even if that agreement occurred many years ago. This is an oft-used weapon of the person who refuses to be flexible. "When I came to this church, you said there would be no scheduled meetings on Saturdays, and I'm going to keep you to your word." Even if that is the best time for everyone else to meet, and though it be only temporarily, the contract-tyrannizer will not change behavior.

Trivial tyrannizing is another weapon in the arsenal of dirty-fighting. When resentments build, as they sometimes do when we do not share them early, the trivial tyrannizer will "get back at" the other person by doing little things known to "get that person's goat," behaviors like repeatedly

221

mispronouncing or misspelling a name, or showing up a few minutes late every time an inconvenient meeting is called, or continuously bringing up a sensitive or embarrassing subject, or using certain near-vulgar words and expressions. When a pastor becomes acquainted with the people and politics of the parish, and keeps an ear out for subjects, words, and relationships that irritate others, trivial tyrannizing is a weapon of dirty fighting that is always near at hand and tempting to use.

Personally, I think *withholding* is one of the dirtiest forms of fighting ever devised. The withholder knows the other person well enough to know what that person really appreciates in a relationship; then, as a way to punish the other person for an alleged wrong, the withholder will keep back that which the other likes or wants. In an affectionate relationship, it may mean withholding humor, conversation, sex, courtesy, or time together. Instead of expressing anger or resentment in a way both can deal with it, withholding only increases anger or builds greater resentment. A pastoral withholder (almost seems like a contradiction in terms) may keep back expressions of encouragement, or polite conversation, or become "too busy" to spend time with the people of the parish or with the person or persons at whom s/he is angry or resentful.

Blaming is another dirty weapon often used in conflict management. The blamer is more interested in hurting the other person than in working toward a solution to the problem at hand. Seldom does the blamer blame her/himself, unless it is an indirect way to make the other person feel badly. Sometimes the blamer will lay fault on the situation or on fate; however, that, too, doesn't move toward any kind of solution to the conflict; it only diverts attention. Blaming the other person is the usual way of fighting with this weapon, and it works well in creating a defensive climate. Every parish has people who blame God for their woes (and sometimes even take it out on the pastor!). I have heard numerous examples of blaming at meetings of clergy, when they lay blame for their problems on the recalcitrants in their churches; as I have heard at least an equal number of laypersons blame their church's problems on the pastor. The problem or conflict is never met head on; no solution is found; only time is spent on laying blame.

Beltlining is another weapon on the rack, one especially tempting for the intimate to use. When a person self-discloses to us, that person becomes very vulnerable. We suddenly have information we can use against that person, especially when the self-disclosure is of a personal or sensitive nature. Bringing up that information during a conflict, or mentioning it in the presence of non-intimates, is "hitting below the belt" emotionally or psychologically. Convenient "beltlines" might include past behavior, intelligence, confessed feelings, personality traits, or physical characteristics. Having access to vulnerability makes for tempting attacks when conflicts arise. Again, a pastor, with access to the vulnerability of many in the parish, could be tempted to use a beltline or two when conflicts occur.

Trapping is yet another powerful and dirty method of conflict management. This is a very tempting weapon for successful manipulators to use. It involves setting up the other person to behave in a certain manner, then criticizing that person for doing what was requested. For example: "Let's be totally honest with each other." Then, when the other person does express honest feelings, criticize her/him for having those very feelings. I remember how tempted I was in the sixties to be supercritical of the racist attitudes of a few of my parishioners after urging them to be honest with me. Was I really willing to accept honesty as part of the conflict management process, or was I attempting to maneuver them into a position of vulnerability? I hope the former; but if the latter, I was fighting dirty.

Bach labels the next weapon as the "Benedict Arnold" method of dirty fighting. I prefer to call it *betraying*, the process of hurting someone by failing to defend that person from outside attack. Encouraging others outside the relationship to think less of the person we want to hurt by putting her/him down or by public ridicule or striking out

224

at the other person when s/he is in no position to fight back are examples of betraying. Talking derogatorily about the parish to other members of the clergy at a district conference or betraying confidences within the fellowship are two examples of how pastors could employ this weapon of dirty fighting in their conflict management.

The final weapon in the arsenal of dirty fighting that Adler and Towne highlight from Bach's work is called, for want of a better term, *kitchen sink fighting.* This is bringing into a conflict situation topics and behaviors that are totally off the subject ("everything but the kitchen sink" syndrome). In the local church a conflict might arise over changing the weekly times for public worship during the summer months. If someone threw into the argument a statement about the hours of the public library or something a long-deceased grandmother believed or the less pungent odor of altar flowers at the suggested time, that person might be guilty of kitchen sink fighting. Such a method of conflict management is not beyond the imagination of anyone who has attended administrative board meetings!

Dirty fighters are not limited to wielding only one weapon at a time; they usually employ them in combination as they push toward their goal of winning the battle. In all probability there are more weapons than these seventeen described, the number limited only by the creative imagination of

225

the fighter. As Bach suggests, each is designed to "drive the other person crazy;" however, not necessarily to solve a problem or resolve the conflict, but primarily to win the battle with the least cost to the self and the most cost to the other.

Robert Hopper and Jack Whitehead, Jr., authors of <u>Communication Concepts and Skills</u>, in their discussion on conflict management, point out that many conflicts will not move toward resolution unless "reframing" (a term coined by Paul Watzlawick in his book <u>Change</u>) occurs, a process which involves the altering of perceptions. When the combatants see the conflict in a different light, many times the conflict is either diminished considerably or gone completely. Hopper and Whitehead suggest that the American custom of a surprise party might be a valid example of reframing.

> The party is a kind of practical joke in which friends scheme to trick somebody into going to some routine occasion and the subject suddenly finds himself or herself at a place where friends jump out and yell "Surprise." At the moment that the subject realizes what has really been going on, the situation is reframed. Strange things that the friends have been doing are recognized as part of the plot. Reframing thus offers a new theory to explain events.

Hopper and Whitehead then apply reframing to an example with which many of us in the clergy have had experience: marital counseling.

How does reframing apply to conflict? If a situation in which conflict may escalate out of control can be changed into a different kind of situation, violence may be averted, and the parties may even work toward a problem-solving atmosphere. For instance, a married couple argues every day. They do not get enough sleep, their sex life deteriorates, and they act nasty to each other. They seek marriage counseling. The counselor listens to their complaints and informs them that they argue so much because they really care deeply for each other. If they regard arguing as a sign of their special relationship, there is no need for them to be defensive or to worry about who wins the fight. The important thing is that the fight itself takes place and thus reaffirms their relationship. . .A new definition of the situation has been offered that changes the meaning of some of the fight behaviors and makes it possible for the couple to engage in problem solving.

Philip Graham, in his article titled "A Writer in a World of Spirits" in the <u>Poets & Writers</u> magazine, tells of an experience which describes very well the reframing phenomenon. His wife, Alma Gottlieb, a cultural anthropologist, and he were living with the Beng people, a little-known ethnic group in Ivory Coast. As Alma studied the culture, Philip spent his time at the typewriter working on some manuscripts, his being a professional writer. The Beng people couldn't understand what he was doing, sitting there quietly scribbling down notes and tapping away on a strange machine. They interrupted him frequently, often inviting him to join them in productive activities: their farming tasks in the fields. Only much later, by reframing, did they begin to understand what he was doing, the process begun in an interview session between Alma and an animist priest by the name of Kokora Kouassi.

During one of their sessions, Kouassi told Alma of the different sorts of objects diviners can employ to attract spirits—red cloth, white powder, small statues. Drawn to these objects, spirits then speak to diviners, revealing the causes of an illness and who is bewitching whom. Diviners, Kouassi said, are the point where the spirit and human worlds communicate.

As Alma was writing this down, I remarked, "It sounds a bit like what a writer does. We hear voices too."

"Right," she agreed, turning to Kouassi. "That's like what Kouadio (Philip) does."

"Kouadio?" he replied, his eyes squinting and skeptical in the dark room.

"Yes," Alma said, suddenly excited, "voices try to tell him their stories. And that's what he writes down."

"And my paper, and pen. . ." I said to her, and she understood.

"His paper and pen and typewriter," she repeated to Kouassi in Beng, "these are what he uses to draw the voices to him."

Kouassi watched me carefully, as I sat with my notebook in hand. I could see he understood. He had often seen me sitting silently in a corner and then suddenly scribbling furiously: a plausible enough sign of possession (by evil spirits).

I turned to Alma, ready to speak, but she was ahead of me. "Yes!" she said to Kouassi, "That's why he shouldn't be interrupted when he's working, because then the voices leave, and their stories can't be written."

The next day when I sat at our desk in the middle of the compound (the Beng people do not trust people who are secretive and work indoors), no one interrupted me while I wrote, for in the eyes of the Beng my typing was now a physical act that revealed a hidden world. . .I wrote for hours, uninterrupted, visited by spirits the Beng could now see. I had finally found in this different

228

society a complementary fit with my own culture, for
what writer would disagree that we are possessed: by
our imaginations, our interior voices, those gifts that
surge up from within. Our characters call us, as we
call them, and from that invisible, intuitive relationship
our stories grow.

The Beng people saw Philip's activities in a
different light. Reframing had occurred.
Interestingly enough, Philip had reframed, too.
What had caused some tension (conflict) in the past
(the polite interruptions) no longer happened—
because people saw the same situation in a different
light, attributing to it a meaning each could
understand within the culture.

Adversaries on some issue who become friends
during their debates often reframe, and as a result
are more able to work their way through difficult
moments. When a couple "falls in love," reframing
takes place; the same events take on different
meaning. We perceive the relationship differently.
When a local church pastor moves into conference
administration or into academia, reframing takes
place. Denominational decisions which create
tension and conflict are seen in a different light,
and the easing of those tensions often depends on
the willingness of the interactors to share a common
reframing. Jesus may have said "Blessed are the
peacemakers," but in the jargon of successful
communication, reframing is often a necessary
prerequisite. Blessed, indeed, are the reframers,
for they allow adversaries to view a common scene

out of which peacemaking becomes possible.

In their discussion on conflict, Hopper and Whitehead include a very interesting and helpful "Proverbs Test," which locates each person in one of five categories of conflict management: problem solving, forcing, compromising, withdrawing, and smoothing. Depending on how a person rates twenty-five fairly well known proverbs as to their desirability of application in conflict situations, the person can identify the approach to conflict management s/he will most likely employ.

I suggest the reader try this Proverbs Test, and identify which of the five behaviors you tend to employ in most conflict situations. I prefer a behavioral approach: rather than using the "desirable/undesirable" scale, I would ask each reader to apply the "I make every effort to do this/I make every effort not to do this" scale. It results in less intellectualizing and hedging.

Proverbs About Interpersonal Conflict

DIRECTIONS: Indicate your opinion of each of the following short proverbs as a conflict strategy. In each case, ask this question: How desirable is this strategy as a method for resolving conflicts? Use the following key, and write the appropriate number in the blank to the left of each proverb.

1 = completely undesirable   4 = desirable
2 = undesirable   5 = very desirable
3 = neither desirable nor undesirable

___ 1 You scratch my back; I'll scratch yours.

___ 2 When two quarrel, he who keeps silent first is the most praiseworthy.

___ 3 Soft words win hard hearts.

___ 4 A man who will not flee will make his foe flee.

___ 5 Come and let us reason together.

___ 6 It is easier to refrain than to retreat from a quarrel.

___ 7 Half a loaf is better than none.

___ 8 A question must be decided by knowledge, not by numbers, if it is to have a right decision.

___ 9 When someone hits you with a stone, hit him with a piece of cotton.

___ 10 The arguments of the strongest always have the most weight.

___ 11 By digging and digging, the truth is discovered.

___ 12 Smooth words make smooth ways.

___ 13 If you cannot make a man think as you do, make him do as you think.

___ 14 He who fights and runs away lives to fight another day.

___ 15 A fair exchange brings no quarrel.

___ 16 Might overcomes right.

___ 17 Tit for tat is fair play.

___ 18 Kind words are worth much and cost little.

___ 19 Seek till you find, and you'll not lose your labor.

___ 20 Kill your enemies with kindness.

___ 21 He loses least in a quarrel who keeps his tongue in check.

___ 22 Try and trust will move mountains.

___ 23 Put your foot down when you mean to stand.

___ 24 One gift for another makes good friends.

___ 25 Don't stir up a hornet's nest.

DIRECTIONS: Now that you have indicated the desirability of each proverb, transfer your rating numbers to the following blanks. The numbers correspond to the proverb numbers. Then add up the numbers in each column.

5. _____	4. _____	1. _____	2. _____	3. _____
8. _____	10. _____	7. _____	6. _____	12. _____
11. _____	13. _____	15. _____	9. _____	18. _____
19. _____	16. _____	17. _____	14. _____	20. _____
22. _____	23. _____	24. _____	21. _____	25. _____

The totals by themselves do not mean very much. What is significant is the comparison of the figures. If one or two categories are much higher than the others, you tend to behave in a conflict according to that behavioral philosophy. If one or two categories are much lower than the others, you tend to shy away from that form of conflict management. Now that you have completed the Proverbs Test, I will describe what the categories are, according to Hopper and Whitehead.

The first column/category is *problem solving.* A higher total in this column means you tend to approach conflict with a "win/win" attitude: "We can manage our differences in a way that is beneficial to both of us. Let's concentrate on the problem and not on beating each other. Let's focus our attention on the issue rather than on each other as a person or combatant, and see what kind of solution our deliberation will create and how it can satisfy both of us." The problem solver resists bringing to the conflict-negotiation an inflexible, mind-already-made-up, pre-determined solution. This person acknowledges the problem or conflict, listens to the other's perception, openly shares her/his own perception, and cooperates in exploring possibilities for mutual satisfaction.

The second column/category is *forcing*. The Forcer brings to the interaction the attitude: "This is the way it is. I'm right and you're wrong. I've already got the solution to our problem and you're going to agree with me one way or another. You might as well accept it peaceably; I'm going to win and you're going to lose." Forcers use power to subdue others, the power of greater intelligence or knowledge, political power, longer experience, age, physical intimidation, hierarchical authority, or any other of the many forms of power available which can result in winning at the expense of the other person's losing.

The third column/category is one of the most misunderstood approaches to conflict management in our culture today: *Compromising*. This approach is based on the "lose/lose" philosophy: "I will give up only as much as you give up. I will make no more concessions than you are willing to make. If I have to give up something, you do, too. We'll meet in the middle, neither of us getting all that we want. I'm willing to settle for half a loaf, if you are." The focus here is on losing; granted, losing as little as possible, but losing nevertheless.

The fourth column/category is called

Withdrawing, and it's based on the attitude: "It's O.K. if you win because I'm willing to lose. I don't want you to be angry with me, so I won't fight and you'll win by default. You may be right anyway; what do I know? I don't want to risk our continuing good relationship by arguing or by insisting on my rights. Do it your way; I'll not argue." Though this may seem like a "Caspar Milquetoast" approach to managing conflict, sometimes losing a fight is very much worth it to the withdrawer, for backing-off may be perceived as more important to the relationship or to the self-concept than aggressively attempting to win.

The final column/category is called *Smoothing.* This label bothers me a bit, for I think it is misleading. The basic attitude with which a smoother approaches a conflict is to deny its existence. "What problem? Do we have a problem? I don't see one. What are you so upset about? Since there's no problem, there's nothing to work out. You'll feel better tomorrow, and then we can talk about whatever is bothering you." The smoother is really a *denier,* managing the conflict by denying its existence, not accepting the other person's perception of a conflict as valid.

To identify one's own conflict style may be helpful, but I'm at least as concerned about movement toward resolution as I am about identification. In other words, in the process of conflict management, how can we most effectively and satisfactorily resolve our differences so we can live together more productively and happily? In an attempt to answer this question, I have taken Hopper and Whitehead's five approaches to conflict management and placed them on an interactive grid, noting where and how they intersect and what the probable results would be.

	Problem Solver (Win/Win)	Forcer (Win/Lose)	Compromiser (Lose/Lose)	Withdrawer (Lose/Win)	Smoother (no problem)
Problem Solver (Win/Win)	*				**Frustration**
Forcer (Win/Lose)		**Ouch!**		*	**?**
Compromiser (Lose/Lose)			*		**?**
Withdrawer (Lose/Win)		*		**Futility**	
Smoother (no problem)	**Frustration**	**?**	**?**		

The asterisks indicate when a satisfactory resolution is likely. Note that there are only four asterisks on the entire grid: when two problem solvers are fighting, when two compromisers are fighting; and when a forcer is coupled with a withdrawer. Two forcers, both with an "I win/you lose" approach, only result in more pain and no resolution (until one becomes a withdrawer or both move toward problem solving or compromising). Two withdrawers in a conflict often experience only futility with their "It's O.K., you win; please, we'll do it your way." The smoother's approach is often the most difficult to work with, and the results to predict, since it is so nebulous. If both deny the existence of a problem or conflict (when there really is one), the result would probably be a continuing blissful avoidance (until one or the other changed to a different approach). A smoother and a problem solver would only build more and more frustration into the relationship as one would say, "We have a problem that needs to be worked out," and the other would communicate, "No, we don't have a problem; there's nothing to be worked out." A smoother and a forcer might have the best of all worlds, with one saying, "We're going to do what I want, whether you like it or not," and the other communicating, "I don't know what all the fuss is about. No problem." However, no resolution can be forthcoming in this relationship, only a status quo management. If that is satisfying to both, so be it.

This grid was created not only for analytical purposes, for looking at conflict interactions and seeing why they are or are not working, and why satisfactory resolution is not forthcoming, but also for proactive purposes, for consciously applying behaviors which will result in conflict resolution. It is my contention that the most effective conflict manager is the one who is willing and able to change styles in any given conflict in order to achieve resolution when such resolution is deemed desirable. The pastor who can identify the other person's conflict style, and move her/his own style to one that is more likely to achieve resolution, will be a more effective pastor, one who is perceived as both a peacemaker and a pastor who is concerned about maintaining a good relationship. Of course, there may be times when a minister cannot in good conscience change styles, for example, to withdrawing when interacting with a forcer, or become a compromiser when it compromises her/ his basic convictions. Having this grid in mind can be very helpful in conflict situations as it provides the pastor with conscious choices: if the issue is worth risking the relationship, the pastor can choose one conflict style or approach; if the relationship is more important than the issue at hand, the pastor can choose a style that will more likely and quickly result in a mutually satisfactory resolution. Visualizing the grid and where the probabilities are for more effective conflict management is an invaluable communication tool for any pastor.

Most of the aforementioned "crazymakers" (as

Bach labels them) or "weapons in the arsenal of dirty fighting" (as I label them) seem to fall into the forcing, smoothing, and withdrawing category-styles of conflict management. One or two might be compatible with compromising. On the other hand, problem solving, by definition, does not involve crazymaking. Problem solving is what both George Bach and Thomas Gordon call "clean fighting" or "fair fighting." Since I've spent so much time and space discussing "dirty fighting," it is important that I describe the main points or steps in the process of the more positive way to manage conflict.

In communication workshops I have conducted for and with corporate managers, hospital personnel, and others in vocational settings, as well as with my college students, a common reaction I receive when presenting "clean fighting" skills is "This doesn't seem like fighting; it's more like discussing, dialoguing, and negotiating." We have been conditioned and enculturated to look on conflict of any kind as undesirable, as something to be avoided, because "nice people don't fight and hurt each other." However, fighting and hurting people do not necessarily go hand in hand. We need to accept the reality of the inevitability of conflict, and the necessity of managing it in some manner. And, we need to learn "clean fighting" skills. If we wish to label them as negotiating, dialoguing, or discussing, to differentiate them from fighting that hurts people, physically, psychologically, or emotionally, then so be it. Whatever the labels, the goal is to manage conflict in the most productive manner.

George Bach suggests an eleven step procedure for fighting fairly. I will attempt to describe each step by applying Bach's "Fight for Growth" to a hypothetical conflict in a local church: a few members of the congregation are circulating a petition to remove the pastor from this church, basing much of their disgruntlement on the pastor's involvement in civic affairs, especially with the minister's well-known liberal point of view and propensity for appearing in the news media. The pastor has heard, via the grapevine, about the petition being circulated, and that one or two members of the liason committee for pastor/parish relationships is involved; however, the problem has never been *officially* raised.

<u>Step One</u>: *Thinking about the problem.* Before approaching the committee, the pastor will spend time mulling over the problem, getting in touch with just exactly what is bothering him about the situation; for example, is it their disagreement with his theology, or their deviousness in trying to get rid of him, or their not coming right out and discussing the problems involved, or his feeling of betrayal, or a question in his mind that this is a smokescreen for some other complaint they might have, or what? Just why is he bothered, and why

239

does he consider the petition a problem?

Step Two: *Making a date.* Instead of complaining behind closed doors, or cornering one or two "non-involved" others and building a case for herself and/or undermining the suspects, the pastor next makes a date with the committee specifically to discuss the problem of the circulating petition. She does not suddenly appear at the next scheduled meeting and demand a hearing; the members of the committee may not be ready to discuss such an important matter. She allows the others time to prepare for the problem-solving discussion.

Step Three: *Stating your problem.* It is critical that the pastor clearly articulate his perception of the problem, taking the time and making the effort to express what he has been thinking in Step One. He might seriously consider wording the problem in this way: "The thing that bothers me most about the circulation of this petition is that some members of this committee, which is entrusted with the responsibility for keeping the lines of communication open between the pastor and the congregation, are involved and haven't brought it out into the open so it can be discussed rationally and officially. When I accidentally discovered the existence of such a petition, I became very angry, defensive, and suspicious of everyone, and I feel very discouraged and hurt by the people I love." Notice that this rather involved statement is heavy with "I" statements, and very light in the use of the "you" word. The pastor has opened himself up to the committee, to those who are involved as well as to those who are not. He has expressed not only his perception of the problem, but also how he feels about it.

Step Four: *Checking back.* Before any discussion of the problem, the pastor requests a restating of the problem by one or two members of the committee, to make sure they heard what she was trying to communicate. "Before we discuss my problem, let's make sure everyone understands what my problem is. What did you hear me say?" Active listening is important in any serious discussion, but it is absolutely crucial when attempting to resolve a conflict. Hurt feelings, guilt, resentment, and hidden agenda all tend to distort a message. This checking back may take several attempts before the pastor is sure she has been understood, and this step should not be rushed. Bach even suggests that when understanding is finally reached, some form of "thank you" should be expressed and appreciation given for making the effort to understand.

Step Five: *Thinking about and wording the request.* The pastor wants more than just to be understood, although that would be appreciated, too. He wants a change in their behavior, and needs to verbalize it so the committee can process it. What exactly does he want? He needs to word the request simply enough that it deals with only the issue at hand. "I want the committee to discuss openly any and all complaints about my ministry here, and to publicly disassociate itself from the unofficial petition being circulated." Such a request is clear, and it involves a behavior, a specific action that the committee can take.

<u>Step Six</u>: *Checking back on the request.* This is a repeat of Step Four, a request for the verification of understanding. In this step, the committee is not being asked to fulfill the request, only to repeat the request so the requestor knows it has been understood. Appreciation might be offered here, as well.

<u>Step Seven</u>: *Popping the question.* It is only after being sure that she is understood, that the pastor asks the committee to do as she is requesting. "Will you do as I ask?" It is important to realize that understanding a request, as important as that may be, is not committing to the request. They are two distinct behaviors. It is tempting and dangerous to assume that because people understand the request for change, that they are committing themselves to doing it.

<u>Step Eight</u>: *Deciding the answer.* Now it's in the committee's lap. The request has been made; it has been understood; what will be its decision? Can the committee do all that the pastor is requesting, or at least some of it? Is it willing to do so? What will be the consequences? At this point, maybe the pastor will want to absent himself, after all

questions for clarification are answered, so the committee can deliberate. (I personally do not think this is either useful or desirable, but in some situations, it may work.)

Step Nine: *Answering the question.* "Yes, we will do as you request." "No, we won't do it." "We'll discuss complaints openly as they are made known to us, but we'll not make any public statement that might give credence to an unofficial petition." (Although Bach doesn't include a checking back step here to make sure the answer is understood, I think it would be very important to insert another one at this point. Then the committee will know that the pastor fully understands what the committee will and will not do.)

Step Ten: *Planning a checkup meeting.* After progressing through a "fight" such as this, it's a good idea to set aside a time later to evaluate the results thus far. At such a meeting, the pastor and the committee will address the questions: "Is our solution working? Are we all still satisfied with our decision?"

Step Eleven: *Closure.* Another very important step often overlooked. Now that the pastor and the committee have successfully worked their way through a "growth fight," they should congratulate each other. A prayer of thanksgiving may be appropriate. A verbalized expression of gratitude for the time and effort made by all may be appreciated, too. Whereas before this meeting there was a conflict and some feelings of resentment, now the focus is on the mutually agreed upon solution.

Bach's eleven steps (and my insertion of a twelfth) may seem very ponderous, and overly organized—not like a "real" fight where we can just let go and be spontaneous! However, this kind of confrontation and dialoguing is much more conducive to positive results, and does not play so much havoc with people's feelings and relationships. One of my students reacted to Bach's approach this way: "This seems like a lot of work just for a fight! It's more work than fun!" Fighting for the thrill of it is one thing; fighting to arrive at a mutually satisfying solution is quite another! Manipulation and crazymaking may work well for thrillseekers; it does not work well for problem solvers. Bach's "fight for growth," on the other hand, does.

A second, and less complex, fair-fighting method of conflict management has been suggested by Thomas Gordon in his book, Parent Effectiveness Training. He calls it a "no-lose approach," and it is obviously based on Dewey's system for rational discussion.

Step One: *Identify and define the conflict.* The pastor in the above conflict with the liason committee would articulate his perception of the problem by using the recommended "I" language rather than the "you" defensiveness-raising language. He would define the end he seeks, putting it in behavioral terms rather than theoretical jargon, and not focus on the means to achieve the end. He would then request the committee members to share their perceptions of the problem and define the ends they seek, again avoiding for the moment any discussion of the means to achieve them.

Step Two: *Generate a number of possible solutions.* The pastor would invite the committee to join him in brainstorming for any and all possible solutions to the defined problem, from the most ridiculous and impractical to the most rational and implementable. Creativity should be encouraged, and, as in all brainstorming sessions, no evaluation of the suggestions should be made until all possibilities are before the group.

Step Three: *Evaluate the alternative solutions.* Here the pastor urges the group to look at each and every suggestion, one at a time, weighing the merits of each in a serious manner. Those solutions that obviously will not work are scratched. Those that are not appropriate at this time are scratched. Those that will cause more harm than good to the congregation are scratched. When the list of possible solutions has been reduced to maybe three or four, it's time to move on to the next step.

Step Four: *Decide on the best solution.* Here the group picks the solution that it determines will be best for all involved, congregation and pastor. Everyone not only should understand the decision being made but also be willing to support it. It should be further understood that the decision is not necessarily final, as etched in granite; it is the best one available at this point in history, according to the pastor's and the committee's best judgment.

Step Five: *Implement the solution.* In this step the pastor and committee will work out the details of how to put the decision into effect. Who will do what and when? What are the steps to be taken, both within the committee structure and with the congregation at large? It is crucial that everyone in the meeting clearly understand what will happen and when.

Step Six: *Follow up the solution.* After the solution has been tried for a fair amount of time, after it has been tested fairly, it is wise to set up a time to evaluate how it's going. If some changes are deemed necessary, make them. If the whole problem needs rethinking, followup sessions are the time to do it. It is very important to structure followup sessions into the problem solving procedure, for seldom are conflicts so simple that people can visualize ahead every effect and consequence of applied solutions. Unanticipated reactions and responses, as well as new information, need to be addressed and incorporated into solutions that are to be workable over a span of time.

Whether to use Bach's "Growth Fighting" system or Gordon's "No-Lose Solution" approach or some other fair fighting method of conflict management is, of course, the choice of every pastor. The two I have outlined are known to work, have been tested successfully by many people, and are now listed under the "tried and true." Certainly, Bach and Gordon have not exhausted the possibilities. To personally design a system of problem solving and conflict management, one that would include the clean fighting skills in each of Bach's and Gordon's approaches plus one's own unique talents and communication strengths, might be a challenging task and one well worth the time and effort. Since no pastor can escape conflict in the ministry, it being both natural and even necessary for growth, to know how to manage these conflicts effectively and constructively is one of the most important skills any pastor can possess.

One final word on conflict. Sometimes pastors feel such enormous tension and great pressure because of the multitude and/or intensity of conflicts in their lives that it's almost impossible for them to think beyond the immediate discomfort to *solving* the problems that have caused this excessive pressure. Like a person with a painfully expanding boil under the skin, relief will come only when the pressure is released and all that pent-up poison explodes. Fortunate is the pastor who knows someone willing to hear the explosion, but not take it personally or think less of the pastor because of this need for relief. At such a time, the wise and caring pastor will prepare the listener with words such as these: "I'm going to blow my top. There's just too much tension. I'm feeling more pressure than I can bear. Please don't take it personally. I don't want to solve any problems right now. I just want to yell!" Then let it out. Problem solving can come later-—after the tension is relieved. But it is only fair to warn the other person of what is coming. Someone once called this "having a Vesuvius." Maybe a more modern expression would be "St. Helen's again!" or "Here goes another Pinetubo!"

Since we humans are choicemakers, we choose how we will behave in conflict situations. We can choose to manage our conflicts in a predominantly rational manner, or with a more spontaneous expression of emotion, or with a systematic combination of both. Whatever we choose to do, we will be managing these conflicts, sometimes moving towards resolution, and sometimes not. The pastor who has analyzed and evaluated her/his own style, who avoids behaviors which can escalate the conflict, and who is aware and makes use of alternative behaviors which can turn potentially destructive situations into opportunities for interpersonal growth, will be a more respected leader and sought-after peacemaker than one who remains blissfully ignorant of the possibilities of ministry in the management of conflict.

Postscript to Volume One

If a pastor understands these communication basics and assimilates them into her/his personality and relationships, s/he will most certainly have a more satisfying and effective ministry. For a behavior we thought so natural and simple, communicating with others has been discovered to be ever so complex and mystifying. If the reader is still wedded to the cliche, "Just be natural; we've been doing it all our lives!", I suggest rereading Chapter One as a starter. Communicating is one of the most misunderstood and misused behaviors humans do, and it is one of the most misunderstood and misused opportunities we pastors have as we perform our ministry. As I have indicated earlier, we need both a heightened awareness of this process and systematic practice in applying positive communication skills to our pastoral leadership. It is to this end that I have written this all-too-brief two volume work. I invite and challenge groups of pastors to sit down together, in workshop and seminar settings, with competent, experienced, and committed communication guides and leaders, and discuss the content of these chapters, bringing to the gatherings their own insights and experiences with these topics for the benefit of each and for the glory of God.

Chapters One through Nine (Volume I) have sought to provide the basics of communication for the reader. Chapters Ten through Fifteen (Volume II) will attempt to place these basics in the kinds of situations ministers commonly find themselves. These volumes are being written to stand alone, and can be studied and discussed apart from the other; however, they probably will make more sense being read sequentially: "basics" first, followed by "situations."

Acknowledgements & Permissions

Scripture quotations are from the *New Revised Standard Version of the Bible*. Copyright 1989 by the Division of Christian Education of the National Council of the Churches of Christ in the USA. Used by permission. All rights reserved.

Experiences 3.4 & 6.6 and Examples on p. 149 from *Communication Concepts and Skills* by Robert Hopper and Jack L. Whitehead, Jr.. Copyright © 1979 by Robert Hopper and Jack L. Whitehead, Jr. Reprinted by permission of HarperCollins Publishers, Inc.

Excerpts from *Looking Out, Looking In: Interpersonal Communication* by Ronald B. Adler and Neil Towne, copyright © 1975 by Holt, Rinehart and Winston, Inc., reprinted by permission of the publisher.

Adler, Ronald & Neil Towne. *Looking Out, Looking In.* 2nd ed. (Fort Worth, Texas: Holt, Rinehart and Winston, 1978).

Excerpts from *Looking Out, Looking In: Interpersonal Communication*, Sixth Edition by Ronald B. Adler and Neil Towne, copyright © 1990 by Holt, Rinehart and Winston, Inc., reprinted by permission of the publisher.

Adler, Ronald & Neil Towne. *Looking Out, Looking In.* 7th ed. (Fort Worth, Texas: Harcourt Brace Jovanovich College Publishers, 1993).

Excerpts from *Interplay: The Process of Interpersonal Communication*, Fourth Edition, by Ronald B. Adler, Lawrence Rosenfeld, and Neil Towne, copyright © 1989 by Holt, Rinehart and Winston, Inc., reprinted by permission of the publisher.

Excerpts from *Interplay: The Process of Interpersonal Communication*, Fifth Edition, by Ronald B. Adler, Lawrence Rosenfeld, and Neil Towne, copyright © 1992 by Holt, Rinehart and Winston, Inc., reprinted by permission of the publisher.

Bach, George. *Aggression Lab: The Fair Fight Manual.* (Dubuque, IA: Kendall-Hunt Publishing Company, 1971).

Bormann, Ernest, William Howell, Ralph Nichols, George Shapiro. *Interpersonal Communication in the Modern Organization.* 2nd ed. (Englewood Cliffs, New Jersey: Prentice-Hall, 1982). Model reprinted by permission from Allyn & Bacon.

Cleaver, Eldridge. *Soul on Ice.* (New York: Dell Publishing Company).

Gibb, Jack R., "Defensive Communication." *Journal of Communication*, Vol. 11, No. 3, 1961. Used by permission.

Gordon, Thomas. *Parent Effectiveness Training: The Tested New Way to Raise Responsible Children.* (New York: Peter H. Wyden, 1970).

Graham, Philip, "A Writer in a World of Spirits." *Poets & Writers*, Vol. 17, No.3, 1989. Used by permission.

Huxley, Aldous. *Collected Essays.* (New York: Harper & Row Publishers, 1959).

Luft, Joseph. *Group Processes: An Introduction to Group Dynamics.* (Mountain View, CA: Mayfield Publishing Company). Used by permission.

Meerloo, J.A.M. *Conversations and Communication.* (Madison, CT: International Universities Press). Used by permission.

Martin, Judith. *Miss Manners' Guide to Excruciatingly Correct Behavior.* (New York: Simon & Schuster, Inc., 1982). Used by permission.

Wells, Theodora, "An Experience in Awareness." *Newsletter: Association for Humanistic Psychology* VII-3, December, 1970. Used by permission.

Additional Selected Readings

Bach and Goldberg. *Creative Aggression.*

Bach and Wyden. *The Intimate Enemy.*

E. Berne. *Games People Play: The Psychology of Human Relationships.*

K. E. Boulding. *Image: Knowledge in Life and Society.*

Condon and Yousef. *An Introduction to Intercultural Communication.*

V. E. Frankl. *Man's Search for Meaning.*

E. Fromm. *The Art of Loving: An Inquiry into the Nature of Love.*

E. Goffman. *The Interaction Ritual: Essays on Face-to-Face Behavior.*

—. *The Presentation of Self in Everyday Life.*

E. T. Hall. *The Hidden Dimension.*

—. *The Silent Language.*

T. A. Harris. *I'm OK, You're OK: A Practical Guide to Transactional Analysis.*

S. I. Hayakawa. *Language in Thought and Action.*

E. Hoffer. *The True Believer.*

James and Jongeward. *Born to Win: Transactional Analysis with Gestalt Experiences.*

S. M. Jourard. *The Transparent Self: Self-Disclosure and Well-Being.*

J. W. Keltner. *Interpersonal Speech Communication.*

M. Knapp. *Nonverbal Communication.*

J. Lair. *I Ain't Much, Baby—But I'm All I've Got.*

W. Lutz. *Doublespeak.*

A. Maslow. *Toward a Psychology of Being.*

R. May. *Love and Will.*

—. *Man's Search for Himself.*

A. Mehrebian. *Nonverbal Communication.*

K. A. Menninger. *Love Against Hate.*

A. Montagu. *Touching: The Human Significance of the Skin.*

Nichols and Stevens. *Are You Listening?*

J. Pearson. *Gender Communication.*

J. Powell. *The Secret of Staying in Love.*

—. *Why Am I Afraid to Tell You Who I Am?*

H. Prather. *Notes to Myself.*

C. Rogers. *On Becoming a Person.*

Rogers and Stevens. *Person to Person: The Problem of Being Human.*

V. Satir. *Peoplemaking.*

E. L. Shostrom. *Man, the Manipulator: The Inner Journey from Manipulation to Actualization.*

M. J. Smith. *When I Say No, I Feel Guilty.*

J. Stewart (ed.). *Bridges Not Walls: A Book About Interpersonal Communication.*

D. Tannen. *That's Not What I Meant!*

A. Toffler. *Future Shock.*

253